MW00619625

THE ART OF BEING PRESENT

Mindfulness Meditation for Work and Life

The
ART of
BEING
PRESENT

Mindfulness Meditation
for Work and Life

by Edie Raphael, PhD

RED LIZARD PRESS

Published by Red Lizard Press
West Linn, Oregon

Library of Congress Control Number: 2018952447

ISBN 978-0-9970174-7-2

The Art of Being Present: Mindfulness Meditation for Work and Life / Edie Raphael

Cover photo by Chris Barbalis on Unsplash.
Cover design by Stephanie Wetherby.
Photo credits listed on pages 168-169.

Printed in the United States.

To all of the courageous people who have sat with me for ten minutes in the middle of their hectic day to find a few moments of respite from the strain and pressure of their work and life.

To my mother, Phyllis, who would have loved meditation had she found it in her lifetime.

To my father, Robert, who does not like or understand meditation but loves me with his entire heart and soul.

And to my own children, Parker and Naomi, who inspire me every day to be a better person.

CONTENTS

INTRODUCTION

A few years ago, while filling my car at a gas station, a professionally dressed woman on the other side of the pump peeked her head around and asked if I could help her. The problem, she explained, was that in her rush she had pushed too many buttons too quickly and now the machine was completely unresponsive — frozen.

"Sure," I replied. "The solution," I explained, "is to do nothing. Just wait a minute and the machine will reset."

So, the woman waited and a minute later the machine reset. "You were right," she chuckled.

"Yes," I replied. "It's a classic case of 'don't just do something, sit there.'"

"Don't just do something; sit there," she repeated. "I really like that! I'm going to remember that one."

"Yeah, it's a good one," I replied. "Sometimes doing nothing is the most useful thing you can do."

Accomplished people, people who are doers and thinkers, can be very uncomfortable with the concept that sometimes (or maybe often) the best solution to a problem is doing nothing, or doing nothing for a while until a better (or the best solution) comes to mind.

Until I was in my mid-thirties, a mother of two with a PhD after my name and a part-time teaching gig at a prestigious university, I believed in the absolute power of thinking. In fact, I was invested deeply into believing these three simple formulas: "thinking = good," "more thinking = really good," and conversely, "not thinking = bad (really, really bad)."

And then I discovered yoga, mindfulness, and the pursuit of the quieted mind. Initially, I was put off by what first appeared to me as its anti-intellectual, or at least anti-thinking message. But after some period of resistance (actually a long period of resistance), I began to discover the peacefulness of living in the present moment. I had grown up in a wonderful family of professional worriers and spent a lot of time worrying about a future that had yet to unfold and about a past that could not be changed.

Mindfulness was a respite from all of that worry. I remember one day walking my children to school and instead of the typical litany of worries and concerns (would we be late, did I pack enough for lunch, was the front door locked, etc.) I just walked in the peace of the moment: the chill of the fall morning air, the slower tempo of young children, the growling engine sounds from the school buses rolling by. In that moment, I finally understood how my mindfulness practice in yoga could create a peaceful life for me off the mat.

What's the difference between *Mindfulness* and *Meditation?*

People frequently use meditation and mindfulness interchangeably, but there are useful distinctions between the two. In this book, I try to use the terms with precision but sometimes even I conflate the two. Generally speaking:

Meditation is the more generic of the two words. Meditation might be thought of as concentration. We're focusing on, concentrating on, or directing our minds to a particular thing: a thought, a phrase, a visual image, body part, movement, or sensory information.

Mindfulness refers to our relationship with the present moment. Jon Kabat-Zinn, arguably the founder of the modern mindfulness movement, defines mindfulness as "paying attention in a particular way: on purpose, in the present moment, and nonjudgmentally." [1] A person can be mindful in any given situation—while eating, driving the car, petting a dog, or even engaging in a conversation—as long as the mind is fully aware of what is happening in the moment and not lost in thoughts.

The work of being mindful is about slowing down and being present. Like the woman at the gas station, we're all in a hurry trying to squeeze more life out in the shortest amount of time. And yet, it's the hurry and worry that actually slows us down, makes us unhappier, and less productive.

This book is fundamentally about the power of mindfully doing nothing. Meditation is essentially just that. In meditation, we sit and become aware of the present moment as it unfolds, neither changing nor judging what is unfolding.

Why is mindfulness powerful?

The answer to that question is multifold. The ancient people living in the Indus Valley who first practiced meditation five to seven thousand years ago would have a different answer than today's scientists using fMRIs to map how the brain responds and changes. But even without advanced technology to help them understand the effects of meditation, early practitioners had a keen awareness of how the practice made them happier and more peaceful. In the Bhagavad Gita, it is written:

> *The yogi who has completely calmed the mind and con-trolled the passions and freed them from all impurities, and who is one with Spirit—verily, he has attained supreme blessedness.*

Today we have science to back up the observations of the ancients and to add even more to the list of meditation's benefits. The science on mindfulness is rapidly evolving. So much so that it's likely that by the time you read this book, the science supporting mindfulness will have grown far more robust.

To date, research published in top medical journals has identified at least eight different regions of the brain which are dramatically changed in as little one session of mindfulness practice. Here are just some of the documented benefits of mindfulness which have captured the attention of executives and corporations.

Productivity

The practice of mindfulness…

Improves ability to focus and pay attention

In the busy world of business, the ability to stay focused on the task at hand is key. MRI scans of meditators show more stability in their ventral posteromedial cortex (vPMC)—a region linked to spontaneous thoughts and mind-wandering. And on both brain scans and performance studies, meditators are shown to have quieter "resting" brain activity and a heightened ability to focus.[2] In a study from UC Santa Barbara on the effects of mindfulness on focus and memory, researchers divided students studying for the GRE into two groups. One group was rigorously taught nutritional tips for improving health while the other was similarly schooled in mindfulness techniques. The group which learned and practiced mindfulness meditation increased their GRE scores by an average of 60 points.[3] The nutrition group saw no increase.

Boosts working memory

Whether you need help remembering the names of your clients or where you set down your phone, working memory can save you time and increase productivity. Studies have shown that after eight weeks of daily meditation practice meditators increased the thickness of their hippocampus—the site of working memory.[4] The American military community (especially the Marine Corps) has been exploring the benefits of mindfulness before and after combat experience.[5] One study of highly stressed pre-deployment military groups who participated in an eight-week mindfulness meditation training showed significant advantages in working memory over their peers who did not participate.[6]

Increases information processing and improves decision-making

For everyone in management, complex decision-making and information processing with speed are valuable assets. People who practice mindfulness are better at framing decisions (in the context of goals, values and needs), gathering relevant information, coming to a conclusion with speed and confidence, and learning from feedback in the aftermath.[7]

Scientists have observed that long-term meditators have larger amounts of gyrification ("folding" of the cortex, which may allow the brain to process information faster) than people who do not meditate. Furthermore, a direct correlation was found between the amount of gyrification and the number of meditation years, possibly providing further proof of the brain's neuroplasticity, or ability to adapt to environmental changes.[8]

Health Benefits

The practice of mindfulness also…

Reduces workplace injury

The insurance giant, Aetna, reported a decline in health care costs and Green Mountain Coffee saw injury rates drop among factory workers when company-wide mindfulness programs were instituted.[9] The reason might be that mindfulness increases attention span and focus, thereby reducing injuries caused by distractions and lack of attention.

Decreases level of anxiety, stress and depression

A mindfulness practice called Mindfulness Based Cognitive Therapy (MBCT) has been found in multiple studies to reduce depression and anxiety as much as prescription drugs.[10,11] Mindfulness accomplishes this by allowing practitioners to take control of their perseverating over negative thoughts, experiences and memories. By disciplining the mind through mindfulness, people prone to depression are able to actively stop the repetition of negative self-directed thinking.

Reduces the risk of heart attack and stroke

In a five-year study focused on African Americans, the American

Heart Association found that participants practicing meditation twice daily were 48% (yes, you read that right) less likely to experience a heart attack or stroke.[12]

Decreases inflammation

Researchers are exploring whether meditation practice can help reduce chronic inflammation. One study found that a brief mindfulness meditation-based stress-reduction intervention helped patients with psoriasis.[13] Other studies have found links between MBI (Mind Body Interventions—which emphasize mindfulness) and a decrease of genes associated with higher levels of inflammation.[14]

Decreases alcohol and substance abuse

The NIH has reviewed a large body of well-executed studies on substance abuse and addiction which have shown that various mindfulness-based strategies help significantly reduce addiction by lowering stress-induced relapses.[15]

With all of the benefits of mindfulness, it's clear that meditation profits everyone. This book, however, is particularly aimed at successful, busy people who thus far have lived their lives constantly thinking and doing, and all the while not finding peace. Many of the writings here will speak universally, but many address the specific challenges faced by folks who struggle with the enormous challenges of work-life balance, whom others depend on for their own livelihood, who miss bathroom breaks and lunch due to the demands of work—workplace warriors, I call them. It is these folks who need mindfulness meditation the most.

Getting Started on Your Personal Practice

If you're on board so far with the idea that meditation can improve your life (and who amongst us doesn't need a little—or a lot of—improvement), then you might be wondering how you can get started.

Before we get to the specifics of how to set up your practice, it's important to consider that there are many obstacles to being mindful. The main one is that your brain has evolved to always be in a state of "on." Being able to evaluate what has happened in the past and plan for the future is what saved our genetic ancestors from being eaten by bears. If that cave you pass on the way to the berry bushes has a bear in it, and that bear gave you quite a run for your life this morning, then you're more likely to survive if you avoid walking by that cave in the future. Even though thinking about past and present was, and still is, helpful to surviving, like all good things it comes at a cost. By not being in the present moment more often, we're prone to host of disorders and diseases, such as stress, anxiety, depression, and overeating, for example.

This tendency to perseverate on the past and get lost in planning out your future has become the default mode of our brain. Some people call it "stream of consciousness"; scientists referring to the neural pathways observed on fMRIs call it the default-mode network.

In order to overcome your brain's deeply entrenched patterns of operating, you will need a consistent practice, and consistency comes down to ease and commitment. Remember, you're up against thousands of years of brain evolution here. The good news is that the brain is fairly malleable (what scientists calls neuroplasticity) and it is capable of changing its patterns. With a regular ongoing practice, the parts of your brain that track the current moment experience (the present-moment pathway), get stronger.

How is a regular ongoing practice defined? What a consistent practice looks like depends somewhat on you. Most of the research on the benefits presumes a daily practice, and indicates that the more you meditate the more benefits you accrue. Scientists seem to have homed in on a daily practice of at least twenty minutes; however, we can't let ideals get in the way of our practice. **It is helpful to consider that the best approach to practicing is whichever one you're most likely to do.**

It may, in part, come down to ease. Make it as easy to start and maintain a practice as possible. You might want to begin with a commitment to meditate two to three times per week for five to ten minutes. Start with small wins and then build gradually, over time, eventually committing to a regular practice six to seven times per week, for fifteen to twenty minutes at a time. Also consider ease when planning *when* in your day to meditate. The best time to meditate is whatever time is most conducive for you to have a regular consistent practice. If you can, try to find time first thing in the morning (before you get on electronics or engage in long conversations), when the mind is least active. A morning sit also helps you set the tone for your day. However, if you find that mornings don't work for your schedule, try to find a time when you can consistently practice without interruptions. And if you miss your regularly scheduled time, no worries. Just pick the next available time.

The best *place* to practice is wherever you will actually practice. Years ago, I set up a lovely, quiet space in my basement for yoga and meditation, but I found that getting myself down there (especially in the cold winter months) required effort that often impeded my practice. So instead, I purchased a meditation bench for my bedroom floor and that's where I sit most days. I'd say that if the best place for you to practice is sitting up in bed after you wake up, then as long as you are sitting upright, that's a fine place to practice. The location doesn't need to be in a sound-proof chamber, but ideally, it should be reasonably quiet. Keep the lights low or just use natural light. Consistency in location is helpful as it reinforces the association of a particular space with a particular mindset (present-mindedness).

By setting up your practice with an eye toward ease, commitment encounters less resistance. As with any new commitment or habit, it's helpful to keep the beneficial outcomes in mind. If you are meditating because you want to lower your stress levels, call upon visual images of the benefits of decreased stress whenever you feel yourself wavering in your commitment. You can summon an image of a blood pressure cuff with a low blood pressure reading, an image of yourself twenty years from now looking healthy as you age, an image of you at your desk being more productive, or an image of your children who benefit by having a calmer, happier parent when you meditate. Another method of boosting your commitment is to create a reward system. Consider a chart in which you get the satisfaction of hitting your goals or something tangible or experiential, such as day trip to your favorite local getaway or purchasing an item you've been eyeing for weeks.

How to Meditate

Once you've set up a location, time, and frequency, now what? What exactly is meditation and how do you do it? Going back to Jon Kabat-Zinn's definition of mindfulness—paying attention in a particular way: on purpose, in the present moment, and nonjudgmentally—we can see the blueprints for our practice: intentionally bringing awareness of the present moment to the forefront of our minds, and observing the present moment without judgment of what is happening in it.

Here are some general instructions for your day-to-day mindfulness meditation.

It helps to set a timer of some kind either on your phone, or even better, on a timing device that is not linked to the internet. If you are using your phone, turn it to airplane mode.

When setting up to meditate, find a comfortable place to sit. If you sit on the floor you might find it helpful to put a pillow or cushion under your hips. You don't need to sit with your legs crossed or in lotus pose, just sit in such a way that you are comfortable and your posture signals a sense of alertness, i.e. keep your spine long. If you sit in a chair, make sure to place your feet fully on the floor for a sense of stability or grounding through the feet.

Once you have found your seat, close your eyes gently or keep them open with soft downward gaze. Take a moment or two to notice the darkness with the eyes closed. Then take a few deep breaths, noticing the lungs fill and empty.

Now spend a few moments scanning the body for any areas where you are holding in tension. Bring a sense of softening and letting go to the places where you feel tightness and clenching: feet, legs, belly, hands, shoulders, neck, jaw and brows.

For the remaining minutes, simply bring your mind to the present moment experience, noticing what is happening, moment by moment, without any judgment of yourself or what you are experiencing. Every time your mind wanders, as soon as you are aware that it is doing so, bring it back to the present moment (again, without judgment). Simple but not easy. Remember we are slowly training our minds to be more present than they have been programmed to be over the course of human evolution.

These are the basics of any mindfulness meditation practice. Along the way, this book will offer variations you can use to expand or deepen your meditation experience. Different meditation techniques offer different benefits, and this book will expose you to the most commonly used techniques so you can get the full range of life-changing outcomes.

How This Book Works

The book is intended to accompany you on your year-long journey with a regular meditation practice. In the pages that follow, you will find over 52 weekly reflections on mindfulness practice that are meant to take you through a full year, plus a few extras. These reflections include tips on how to practice, reminders of the many benefits of mindfulness, and seasonally specific themes. The reflections are organized into six sections: 1 – Getting Started, 2 – Going Deeper, 3 – Mindfulness for Work, 4 – Reflections for Personal Development, 5 – Deepest Reflections, and 6 – Seasonal and Holidays.

The "Getting Started" section is a good place for everyone to start, even if you already have a mindfulness meditation practice. Given that the idea of meditation varies widely from person to person, this section lays out the basic techniques you can use for the entire year. "Going Deeper" takes you further into the practice, offering different accessible mindfulness techniques for quieting the mind and staying motivated. "Mindfulness for Work" focuses on the benefits of mindfulness practice for greater workplace success, and "Reflections for Personal Development" takes a look at how mindfulness improves your emotional and relational well-being. "Deepest Reflections" offers more advanced or esoteric concepts and practices. It's the section we build up to by the end of our year of practice. Finally, the section called "Seasonal and Holidays" is meant to be inserted into your weekly practice at those specific times of the year. Not every season or holiday is included here, just those for which there is a solid link to, or a likely effect on, your practice.

You can start any time in the calendar year, and your mindfulness weeks can begin on any day of the week. For example, you could begin your work with this book the second week of October on a Thursday, and from there count your weeks as Thursday to Thursday, with Week One of the reflections beginning that Thursday in mid-October.

These days, there are many smartphone apps that may help you in maintaining a consistent meditation practice. This book is completely consistent in its message and techniques with the most widely used and accepted apps. *The Art of Being Present* will complement any meditation practice you already do or plan to begin.

Before you turn the page to begin your first week, take a moment to congratulate yourself on taking the first (or next) step toward creating a healthier, happier, smarter, more productive and kinder you.

Quick Summary

Start small — Commit to meditating for ten minutes in the morning or evening, two to three times per week. Over time, you can increase the amount of days and/or minutes.

Make it easy — You don't need to build a meditation annex to the house; just find a quiet spot in your bedroom, office or another out-of-the-way place. Use your phone as your timer. There are apps you can download (such as Insight Timer and Headspace) to help familiarize yourself with meditation techniques, and many meditation techniques will be offered throughout this book.

Create a comfortable seat—Sit on a chair or the floor in a manner that allows your spine to stay long. If you sit on the floor, place a pillow or yoga block under your hips to keep them higher than your knees.

Remind yourself why—At those times when sitting still seems like the last thing you want to do, being very clear about the benefits can be the key to maintaining your practice.

Section 1

WEEKS ONE THROUGH EIGHT

Getting Started

WEEK ONE

The Beginning

When undertaking a new personal practice like mindfulness, it's important to remember for whom you are practicing. We are never practicing for just ourselves. We are also practicing for the important people in our lives: our children, parents, partners, colleagues, friends, and the random people we interact with every day in little or important ways.

Jon Kabat-Zinn, a leader in the western mindfulness movement, defines mindfulness as "paying attention in a particular way: on purpose, in the present moment, and non-judgmentally."[16] One of the most powerful components of his description of mindfulness is non-judgment. From what should we withhold judgment? When we sit quietly, we might become aware of sounds, thoughts, or feelings which either trouble or please us. Our job is simply to notice them without labeling them as "good" or "bad."

One day I was leading a corporate session of mindfulness and we had decided to sit outside. In the background, we heard birds singing, water lapping against the harbor wall, and leaves softly rustling in the wind. In the middle of the session, we began to hear the sound of a heavy building door repeatedly slamming shut. I immediately began to judge that sound as negative. Then I wondered, what if that door opening and closing was the sound of someone I loved walking out to see me? How would it sound to me then? At that moment, I realized that we can sit and experience anything in the present moment without labels or judgment and just notice what is.

For whom are you practicing today?

What do you hope to gain for yourself from the practice of meditation?

What do you hope to give to others through your practice?

WEEK TWO

Real Questions About Meditation

These five questions come from employees at a multi-billion dollar international company who had recently begun participating in a weekly meditation program to reduce stress.

Q) What am I supposed to be doing while I'm meditating?
A) Focusing your mind on the present moment experience, whatever that is.

Q) Can I move while I'm meditating?
A) While there are many forms of being mindful (bringing your mind to the present moment) which include movement, generally speaking, a seated meditation is meant to be held in stillness. As we are trying to settle the mind, we are trying to settle the body.

Q) Even if I have to scratch an itch or adjust my posture?
A) Yes, especially if you have to scratch an itch or shift your weight. In meditation we are teaching ourselves to accept without judgment anything that is happening in the present moment, without wishing it to be eliminated or altered.

Q) I noticed after the session that I was having neck pain. Why?
A) It could be that your efforts at good posture are overzealous and you're holding your head or neck in a funny position. But more likely it's that by slowing down and tuning into the present moment, you noticed something (a feeling or other sensation) that was already there. It's akin to being so busy you don't realize that you're hungry until you get home from work.

Q) My mind keeps wandering the whole session. What am I doing wrong?
A) Nothing. Your human mind is designed to wander. It's the discipline of returning it again and again to the present moment that is the practice of meditation and which yields the benefits. Practice makes practice.

What question(s) do you have about your meditation practice at this stage?

Write them out and see if they are answered as you move through the book.

How to Manage a Busy Mind, Part One

In meditation lingo, a busy, chattering mind is referred to as the monkey mind. There are many days when we all sit down to find quiet and peace but instead encounter the monkey mind. What do you do on those days?

Giving yourself something specific to focus on can help, and focusing specifically on your breathing keeps you fully mindful of the present moment.

Here are two similar methods for counting your breath on those days when your mind is chattering:

Method One: Count forward from one to ten for each full breath (inhale and exhale). If—or when—the mind wanders, just begin counting from the last number you remember or start over again. When you arrive at ten, begin again with one.

Method Two: This method works really well for a very busy mind. Count backward, starting with an exhale at 50, inhale 49, exhale 48, until you get to 20. Then count a whole inhale/exhale as 19, then inhale/exhale 18, etc., until you reach zero. This process can be repeated as many times as you need in order to quiet the mind.

Here are two additional methods for settling the mind, that will help to connect the mind to the body:

Fingertip Focus: Relax your hands in your lap with your palms face up and your fingers curled in a relaxed position. Bring all of your attention to the tip of your right thumb and let it rest there until you begin to feel a tingling sensation there. Shift your attention to the tip of the left thumb, then proceed, moving from right to left through the index fingers, the middle fingers, ring fingers, and finishing with the right and left pinky fingers.

Body Scan: Scan the body from toes to head, inviting relaxation on each exhalation. Begin with the toes on the right foot, then the left foot, then the rest of the right foot, the left foot, and so on, moving from right to left up the body culminating at the head.

Which techniques work best for you?

What did you learn about your mind in these exercises?

WEEK FOUR

How to Manage a Busy Mind, Part Two

When it comes to quieting the mind, there's no one technique that is right or wrong, better or worse. We just try different methods on different days to see what works. This week you can try concentrating on the information picked up by your five senses to bring yourself into the present moment.

As the 80s British band, XTC, explained, we've got five senses working hard all day long. But we're rarely aware of how much information our five senses are constantly signaling to our brain.

Here's how to use your five senses to bring yourself into the present moment.

Sound: After settling your physical body and closing your eyes, home in on your sense of hearing. Pay attention to the sounds you hear in the present moment — those far away and loud, those close by and quiet, and everything in-between. Depending on your location, you might hear sounds of planes in the sky, traffic on the road, voices in other rooms, the hush of air blowing through the ventilation system, a clock ticking, or gurgling in your belly. Keep your attention on the various sounds you are experiencing in each moment.

Sight: Even with your eyes closed, you can utilize the sense of sight to bring yourself into the present moment. Train your inner gaze to the space behind the pineal gland (which sits between the eyebrows). Notice the patterns of light and darkness, paying attention to the shifting of shapes and colors.

Touch: Most of the day, if our day involves being out in public, we are wearing clothing. But we don't notice the sensation of fabric toughing our skin, unless there is an irritant of some sort. We also don't notice the feeling of the pressure of our legs and arms against chairs and tables, or the feeling of air touching skin. For a few minutes, spend time being aware of tactile sensations.

Taste: Unless you've recently brushed your teeth or eaten food, the sense of taste during meditation can be quite elusive. Nonetheless, it's worth being aware of your sense of taste as a way of being more present. Take a few minutes to check in with your sense of taste.

Smell: Finally, spend a few minutes exploring any aromas that you can pick up. Unlike our other senses, our smelling sense fatigues very easily. Give yourself a few minutes of scanning for any scents ("pleasant" or otherwise) that are part of the present moment.

Which of your five senses do you have the easiest access to and which brings you most fully to the present moment?

Which of the five is the hardest for you to access?

WEEK FIVE

Getting Present Through the Body

When you walk into a room or settle into a space to meditate, the only things that might actually be arriving are your skin and bones. The rest of you, especially your mind and your muscles, may be somewhere else entirely. Your mind may be lingering on the work you left on your desk, the conversation you just had, or the deadline that's looming. Your muscles may be holding tension, reflecting your thoughts. There are two helpful techniques you can use to bring your whole self fully present.

Spend the first few moments of your meditation bringing the mind and muscles into the present moment by focusing your attention to relaxing the muscles in the...

feet, legs, hips, belly

hands, arms, shoulders

jaw, mouth, tongue, eyes and forehead.

Remember that in the present moment you are safe and that when your muscles fully arrive with you in the present moment they can reflect your current safe state and relax.

The second technique is to focus your attention on the experience of sitting with your eyes closed and, as if you were an observer, a fly on the wall, to visualize yourself seated in the room. Visualize the space in which you are sitting—perhaps it is a room in a bigger structure. Then visualize the larger structure as if you were observing it from above, from a bird's eye view. Now pan back in again, observing yourself sitting in the room, observing yourself breathing, observing yourself observing yourself.

Where do you tend to hold in tension in your body?

What does it feel like to relax those muscles?

What do you think of the phrase "move a muscle change a feeling"?

What do you feel when you observe yourself breathing?

WEEK SIX

The Science Supporting Mindfulness and Meditation

Welcome to month two of mindfulness! Now is a great moment to remember all of the amazing benefits of the practice which were outlined earlier in the book. Recalling the benefits of the practice will foster consistency and commitment. As you sit down to meditate, you can focus on one particular benefit you wish to cultivate through the practice or feel inspired by the full spectrum of positive outcomes.

Especially when we start losing momentum with our meditation practice, it helps to remember that scientific research has demonstrated that meditation...

Reduces stress and stress-related illnesses. The most well-known and sought-after result from meditation is its ability to reduce the effects of stress on the body — everything from heart disease to psoriasis.[17]

Increases memory and ability to focus, and improves decision-making skills. Really exciting research has demonstrated that mindfulness meditation supports the parts of the brain which affect executive function.[18]

Makes you happier. If reducing stress and increasing brain function aren't enough to make you happy, there's always just happiness itself. Mindfulness meditation decreases anxiety and depression as much as many prescription drugs (without any side-effects).[19,20]

Helps emotional regulation.[21] While the actual mechanism in the brain is still unclear, scientists see a strong connection between mindfulness meditation practice and the moderation of anger impulses.[22]

Buffers against the cognitive decline associated with aging. Along with wrinkles, poorer vision and muscle loss, aging also affects the brain. While meditation isn't exactly a promise of immortality or eternal youth, meditators have been found to have more grey matter than their non-meditating aged peers.[23]

Aids weight loss. People who adopt a mindful eating approach were able to lose weight and to maintain their weight loss very effectively.[24] Eating mindfully is associated with a decrease in stress eating and poor food choices.[25]

Helps manage addiction and substance abuse.[26] Preliminary clinical research, particularly on relapse prevention, suggests that mindfulness can help people with addiction and substance abuse challenges.[27]

With all of these wonderful benefits, you can think of mindfulness practice as your superpower training.

Which benefit of meditation inspires you the most?

What excuses do you use to get out of doing your meditation practice some days?

Make a list and compare the excuses to the benefits.

Which are more important to you?

WEEK SEVEN

Metta (Loving-Kindness) Meditation

The most common distinction made among meditation offerings is guided versus unguided. What we've been doing the past six weeks is what I would call "Introduction to Unguided." But this week we will explore the most familiar of guided meditations: *metta* meditation. *Metta* means "loving-kindness" in the sacred language of Pali. *Metta* meditation is a practice of cultivating loving-kindness to ourselves and others. Many of us walk around with an inner critic in our heads who vocalizes harsh assessments of ourselves and others. The inner critic tells us that we are not enough: smart enough, attractive enough, strong enough, lovable enough, _____ enough (you fill in the blank). In turn, we redirect that inner critic to other people in our lives: our partners, children, co-workers, random people on the internet, etc. *Metta* meditation helps to reprogram our thinking (creating new neural pathways) to silence the inner critic, allowing us to be happier and kinder people to ourselves and to others.

Begin by settling the body in your sitting position for a few breaths. Bring to mind an image of yourself as wholly good and worthy of good things. Maybe you visualize a memory of doing something kind for another person, a pet, or something else. Or bring up an image of yourself as an innocent baby or toddler. Holding that image of yourself in your mind's eye, repeat silently these words:

"May I be safe. May I be healthy. May I be happy. May I be free from unnecessary suffering."

Take your time as you say each line.

Now bring to mind someone you love very dearly: maybe a partner, child, parent or best friend (usually the first person who comes to mind). Holding an image of that person's face in your mind, repeat silently these words:

"May you be safe. May you be healthy. May you be happy. May you be free from unnecessary suffering."

Now bring to mind an image of someone you don't know well and have ambivalent feelings for. It could be the barista who serves your coffee, the guy who works down the hall from you, or the secretary at your kids' school—someone like that, for whom you don't have any strong feelings one way or the other. Holding an image of this person in your mind's eye, repeat the same phrases silently:

"*May you be safe. May you be healthy. May you be happy. May you be free from unnecessary suffering.*"

Now bring to mind someone with whom you have a challenging relationship. Picture this person while you silently say:

"*May you be safe. May you be healthy. May you be happy. May you be free from unnecessary suffering.*"

Now expand your thinking to troubled spots in the world where there is conflict and/or to all sentient beings:

"*May all beings be safe. May all beings be healthy. May all beings be happy. May all beings be free from unnecessary suffering.*"

✳

Reflect on whom it's hardest to send loving-kindness to. For some people it's harder to send loving-kindness to themselves than to loved ones or even virtual strangers.

What about sending loving-kindness to someone you have trouble liking or respecting?

WEEK EIGHT

Establishing a Consistent Personal Practice

For meditation to have the most impact, you need to invest in it regularly. Twice a week is a place to start, but daily is ideal. The best way to have a regular practice is to make meditation a habit like brushing your teeth. We all have routines that are part of getting ready in the morning or going to bed at night. Here are a few guidelines to help you add a regular mindfulness practice to your routine.

Pick the same time each day for your meditation. If you miss that time, practice at the next available opportunity.

Pick a location that is convenient but that also allows you to be uninterrupted for at least ten minutes. Announce to your roommates, family members, or work colleagues your intention to meditate (undisturbed) for ten to twenty minutes, and close the door.

Find an app to keep you motivated or prompt (ping) you to meditate. Some apps will keep track of how many consecutive days you meditate and reward you for your consistency!

Remind yourself why it's important to meditate: happiness, health, relationships, productivity. (See Weeks Six, Nine, Twenty through Twenty-three, and Thirty-one, for example.)

Don't get discouraged if you fall out of the practice. Remember, you can always begin again.

Reward yourself for consistency. After every ten days, find something motivating and healthy with which to celebrate your hard work.

As with any investment, the more you put in the more you get in return.

Do you notice yourself often saying "not now" when you need to make a change in your life?

Do you have conditions which will likely never be met before you will commit to making the change?

At what point in time do you think it will be easier or better to take care of yourself and the people around you?

Section 2

Getting Deeper Into Practice

WEEK NINE

Motivation to Practice

Two months into this practice you may begin to have some deeper questions, such as what's the ultimate point of all of this mindfulness, sitting still, paying attention type of stuff? Is it to become unflappable and Zen-like? Is the final goal to be healthier and happier, or to be a better worker-bee in the hive?

I don't think it's any of that at all. Let's return to the very first reflection from Week One—we practice ultimately for the benefit of others. The aim is to be a better partner, parent, colleague, neighbor (even to the crazy ones next door), and citizen. To the degree that mindfulness enables us to create space in our hearts and minds to find compassion and loving-kindness, embrace humility, be generous, feel gratitude, be honest, and release judgment, stress and resentments, it allows us to be better people.

The desire to suffer less is inherent in the experience of living. The desire for *others* to suffer less exists only in higher orders of and with highly social beings, and it is a hallmark of being human to link the suffering of others with our own. In other words, the best of us suffer when others suffer. An important component, then, of relieving our own suffering is to help relieve others of theirs, especially when we are the cause of it.

When I am impatient or curt with my children, a friend, or a clerk at the store, not only do I create suffering for them, I also suffer with the unkindness of my behavior. When I sit down to meditate, I'm very conscious of the effects of my practice on the other people in my life. Mindfulness is first and foremost a way to end suffering in ourselves and in the world.

How can your practice lead to less suffering in your life?

In the lives of people you deeply care about?

In the lives of people you interact with in casual circumstances?

WEEK TEN

A New Way to Treat the Wandering Mind

Sometimes, when we are meditating, we can become frustrated or feel disappointed by the mind continually wandering.

If we think of our meditation as training the mind to bring itself to the present, then we can see the wandering in a new light. The mind wanders so that we can bring it back; without wandering there's no work in returning it to the present.

A helpful analogy is the image of doing bicep curls with a free weight. Muscle is built not so much by holding the weight close to the shoulder or by the thigh. Instead, the muscle develops in the motion of bringing the weight to the shoulder and then releasing it again.

It's the same with the brain. We are strengthening our cognitive ability to move from the default mode network (the wandering mind) to the present-moment pathway whenever we retrieve the mind from its rambling and bring it back to the present moment.

When my mind is particularly busy, it is sometimes helpful for me to lean into the thoughts. In meditation, the concept of "leaning in" means to get closer to what we are experiencing in the present moment in order to understand it better and then, perhaps, loosening its grip on us. In other words, feelings, sensations, and thoughts can lose their power over us when we sit with them (actually pulling them closer) in a non-judgmental way.

One practice for leaning into thoughts is to name the thoughts as they arise without getting lost in the stories surrounding them. A technique I use is what I call the rolodex method. As you have a thought, name it and visualize it on a card on an old-fashioned rolodex wheel or as the label on a file folder in a cabinet. Instead of falling into the story, visualize flipping to the next card or file. For example, you might have a thought about a meeting in an hour. To avoid the stream of consciousness thinking, simply visualize "meeting" on your card or file and then flip to the next. Sometimes, the same thought keeps showing up on your cards/files. That's normal. Each time, patiently move on to the next thought. In between your thoughts, focus on your breathing.

Were you able to stop the story by turning the card/file?

Did you notice that certain thoughts arrive in your mind repetitively?

What if anything surprised you in your practice this week?

WEEK ELEVEN

How to Greet Unpleasantness

What should you do when unpleasant sensations or thoughts arise in meditation?

When sitting (a frequently used synonym for meditation), it is not uncommon to experience an unpleasant sensation (such as feeling too warm or cold, aching in the hips, back or neck, or a muscle twitching). Unpleasant thoughts or memories can also arise. In both cases the response is the same. We sit with the unpleasantness with a sense of curiosity and patience, asking ourselves to experience it more fully. What does it physically feel like to have a throbbing headache? Where exactly is the ache coming from? Is it constant or intermittent? Or, what precisely does it feel like when I feel anxious, sad, or angry when particular thoughts arise? Are there secondary thoughts which then arise, such as guilt or frustration? How long do the feelings last? Do the thoughts associated with the feelings have a direct connection or are there intermediary thoughts?

This attention is a very different way of responding to unpleasantness. Typically, we try to block out or run away from difficult or troubling experiences, but mindfulness teaches us that there is great benefit in leaning into them. Discomfort and dis-ease are a part of life. If we run away from them, we're in effect running away from a large part of our lives. Sitting with those feelings and thoughts gives us more insight, and thus power to manage them.

There's a story about how the Buddha handled "his demons" just before he became enlightened. As Buddha was sitting under the

If you have experienced significant trauma in your past, it is recommended that you seek the counsel of a trained therapist and meditation teacher.

Bodhi Tree, the demon Mara arrived to thwart his effort at enlightenment. "Who are you to achieve nirvana?" it asked. Rather than running away from or fighting the unpleasant thoughts and emotions, one version of the story has the Buddha inviting Mara to tea.

To invite the unpleasantness to stay and get closer is a more powerful approach than trying to push it away or deny its existence. Spend some time this week leaning into unpleasant emotions, thoughts and physical sensations.

How do you normally engage unpleasantness or discomfort?

What do you notice about them when you explore them more deeply?

WEEK TWELVE

Mindfulness by the Dashboard Lights

Don't have time to meditate? There's an old parable about the meditation guru directing his acolyte to meditate for an hour. The acolyte responds that he doesn't have time to meditate for an hour. "Okay," says the guru. "Then meditate for two hours." The lesson here is that the moment you're too busy to meditate is the moment you need it most.

Still don't think you have ten minutes a day to sit quietly? Try mindful driving. Rather than commuting to work while lost in thoughts, drive while fully aware of what's happening around you. Turn off the radio and listen to the sounds your car makes over different road surfaces and at different speeds. Notice the make, model, and color of the car in front of you. Pay attention to the dance of your right foot as it presses the gas pedal, then the brake, then the gas again (especially in stop-and-go traffic). Also, be conscious of the emotions you are experiencing in traffic (happy, sad, fearful, angry). If possible, open the windows and get a feel for the smells and sensation of the air.

You can also engage in a mindful commute by bicycle or public transportation. Just stay present to the moment as it unfolds, noticing sounds, vibrations, shifts in weight, air currents, sounds, smells, pressure, and textures.

By the way, a driving meditation is a great way to realize how little you pay attention to the present moment in so much of your life. How many times do you arrive at your destination with zero memory of the drive there? It's a metaphor for how we live much of our life on autopilot—just going through the motions and not paying attention. If your work commute is an hour and you're not present for most of the ride, that's at least two out of 24 hours (8%) or two out of sixteen waking hours (12.5%) of your day lost in thoughts.

The commuting mindfulness exercise is great for those days when you need the benefits of mindfulness and don't have the time.

When you practice mindful commuting, what changes for you?

What did you notice/observe that surprised you or felt different?

How did you feel when you arrived at work?

Did you notice any differences in how you felt during the commute and upon arrival?

WEEK THIRTEEN

The Four Foundations of Mindfulness

The tradition of meditation establishes that there are four foundations of mindfulness. Although we've already touched on each of these lightly, over the next four weeks we'll examine the foundations more deeply.

The four pillars of mindfulness are:

- Attention to the sensations of the body in the present moment

- Attention to the feelings and moods in the present moment

- Attention to thoughts in the present moment

- Attention to the wisdom of life revealed in the present moment

This week we'll begin with the first foundation: attention to the sensations of the body.

During our mindfulness practice, we can begin with attention to what lies on the surface of our consciousness and is most accessible: our physical body. You can start with the realization that your bones and skin have entered a physical space called "here." You may notice, though, as soon as you begin to sit still, that some of your muscles are tense and tight as they are carrying remnants of the past or perceptions of the future (stress or anxiousness). Begin to bring the whole body present by working to release any obvious feelings of gripping, tightening, or holding that the body is doing.

Once the body is more present, we begin to lean into the present moment experience of it through awareness of our breath or through our five senses. We can pay attention to the experience of breath through our nostrils (cool air on the intake and warm air on the out). Or focus on the rising and falling in the chest, belly, or ribs as we inhale and exhale.

We can also move through our five senses asking questions or mentally asking, "What sounds are in the present moment?" or noting instead, "I hear sound." "What do I physically feel in the present moment?" "I feel a heavy sensation in my feet right now." "What does it feel like to be tired (or cold, or hungry)?" "What do I smell?" "What do I taste?" "What do I see with my eyes closed?"

And then back to breath. Rising, falling, cool, warm, in, out.

Which sense or body experience brings you into the present moment the fastest?

Which sense is the hardest for you to access?

What did you discover during this practice?

WEEK FOURTEEN

Foundation #2: Feelings and Moods

In addition to paying attention to the body, we need to bring focused attention to the emotions that arise while sitting quietly. This work is not easy. As a psychologist (and yoga student of mine) pointed out, our emotions are always in motion. Figuring out what you're feeling can be like taking aim at a moving target. It helps in the beginning, to be less focused on the words and more on the nature of the feeling. The precise words will come when we gain a precise understanding of the feelings. The key is to stay with the question, "How am I feeling right now?"

Start by taking a broad look and asking yourself if you are feeling good or bad. Then ask yourself what level of good or bad you are feeling (low, medium or high). Keep in mind that you might be tempted to over-report positive emotions or downplay negative. Honesty is the best policy here. Accept what is rather than trying to wiggle into what you want it to be.

The next step is to ask yourself what type of good (accepting, content, hopeful, happy, excited, or elated, for example), or bad (disappointed, nervous, anxious, angry, sad, embarrassed, worried, stressed, depressed).

Finally, explore what it feels like in the body to be angry, sad, stressed, anxious, content, pleased, excited, or happy. Pay attention to how the feelings manifest in the felt body. Where in your physical self do you feel sadness or happiness? Keep asking the questions; keep exploring the experiences.

Being mindful allows us to awaken to the full emotional experience of being alive. The more aware we are of our emotions, the less likely they are to sneak up on us or overwhelm us and wreak havoc on our relationships and careers.

Which emotion do you experience most frequently when you check in?

Where in the body do you experience that emotion?

What does it feel like; what adjectives could you use?

WEEK FIFTEEN

Foundation #3: Thoughts

In addition to checking into the physical and emotional experience of the present moment, we can turn our awareness to our thoughts—the third foundation of meditation.

Even though we are trying to quiet our "monkey mind" in meditation, it's also realistic and helpful to pay attention to the thoughts that do arise while you're sitting. You can notice whether you are thinking about past, future or some simultaneous alternate reality. The rolodex technique (introduced in Week Ten) can be especially helpful in this endeavor. The work of being present to your thoughts happens when you notice and name the subject matter of those thoughts without falling into the story or getting lost in the stream of consciousness which follows.

There are two approaches to becoming aware of your thoughts. The first is to notice them as they naturally emerge (unbidden) while being present. For example, you are focused on breath, watching the chest rise and fall, when all of a sudden a thought about your dinner plans arises. The second approach to thoughts is to actively call them up. We ask ourselves, "What am I thinking about?" Then the thought of dinner comes to mind. You note to yourself, "Oh, I am thinking about dinner." And then you ask yourself, "What else?" And a thought about a childhood experience on the playground comes to mind. You keep the cycle going until your mind settles a little more and you return to the awareness of your breath.

Two other steps can be added to the thought awareness process. As you observe the thoughts that arise, notice which emotions, if any, are attached to those thoughts. Does this thought make me feel good, bad, excited, angry, worried, or embarrassed? Then notice how the feelings that surround that thought get expressed or experienced in the felt body.

By week three you can begin to see how the four foundations are linked to each other.

What thoughts did you notice this week?

Did you notice any trends in terms of whether they were past or future-oriented?

Which emotions were linked with those thoughts?

To what degree did you find that some of your thoughts were on a repeating loop?

Foundation #4: Wisdom of Life

We've arrived at the fourth of the four foundations of meditation. Some call it the mindfulness of *dhamma* (or *dharma*). What is *dhamma*? *Dhamma* is the collective body of truth, wisdom, or "phenomenon" that one observes through the practice of mindfulness. One such phenomena is impermanence — everything is temporary. The wisdom of impermanence is a truth we can observe in our mindfulness meditation practice.

As we sit and notice the sensations of the body, our moods and emotions, and our thoughts, we can observe that they are all temporary. First, we notice that our attention to one thing is fleeting. We sit and our mind wanders from thought to thought or sensation to sensation. If you have an itch on your eye, you might notice that even if you do not react and scratch or rub it, the sensation will eventually go away on its own. People often complain of discomfort in their back, but sometimes if we sit with it and don't move, we might notice the discomfort disappears on its own. It's the same with feelings of fullness, hunger, thirst and hydration.

As the body reflects the wisdom of impermanence, so, too, do our emotions and thoughts. They are always changing in a cycle of emerging, cresting, and then falling away. Feelings of both joy and sadness arise and then give way to another emotion. When we take care to observe our thoughts, we can see that they, too, are temporary. A thought comes up and might stick around for a bit or it might quickly get usurped by another thought. Either way, our thoughts speak loudly about change.

Another related truth we can observe while sitting is our desire to hold on to what is pleasant and push away what is not. When life presents us with something quite enjoyable like new love, delicious food, or a captivating book, TV show or movie, we resist the reality that "all good things must end." At the same time, when life presents us with uncomfortable or painful experiences, we work hard to make the situation end as quickly as possible. The truth can be summed up in the idea that we are naturally inclined to be either in a state of grasping or pushing away.

The *dhamma* teaches us that both of those states cause suffering. The alternative to that suffering is to allow the inevitable change to occur without resisting.

What is something painful in your life right now?

How does noting its impermanence help you manage that pain?

Similarly, note something pleasant in your life right now and reflect on its impermanence.

How does the notion of impermanence affect how you think about things, whether good or bad?

WEEK SEVENTEEN

Overcoming Obstacles to Practice

Have you fallen out of your meditation routine? Maybe someone gave you this book and you tried to practice a few times and decided it's not for you. Well, guess what? Me too!! (Not the book-as-a-gift part, just the not-liking-meditation-at-first part) Give it another try, just like I did.

The bigger the aversion you have to sitting still, the more your mind, body and spirit need it. Your aversion is telling you some important information.

Maybe you've over-trained your doing muscles and now need to give yourself permission to build your non-doing muscles. Our culture overemphasizes the importance of action and often overlooks the importance of resting the body and mind. Doing nothing can feel very challenging (almost painful) to our adult sensibilities. Children have no problem doing nothing all day with little guilt, as many of you, no doubt, have observed in your own homes. But successful adults? Over the years we've trained ourselves to equate action and doing with our sense of self-worth. If we're not engaged in some activity (or two or three) at any given moment, we feel guilty and reproachable. You need to retrain yourself to appreciate the virtues of stillness. Consider this anonymous quote: "Stop the glorification of busy."

Or, you might be avoiding confronting unpleasant thoughts and ideas. Sometimes we don't want to sit in stillness because by slowing down, the thoughts we're trying to avoid come rushing in. Instead of avoiding meditation and unpleasantness, you will feel much better when you sit with and even lean into those thoughts and feelings. Almost nothing gets better when we run away from it. Mindfulness meditation can help us get face-to-face with pain and fear and come away stronger and happier. (See Week Eleven, especially the note for working with trauma.)

You've reached the edge of your comfort zone. I've said it before and I'll say it again: meditation is simple but not easy. In fact, it's really hard. As we know, we often prefer to avoid things that are challenging and that carry no endorphin rush when overcome. Just remind yourself that the more you sit, the easier it gets. Remind yourself, too, whom you are sitting for and how your effort will help others. (See Weeks One and Nine.)

Two quotes for your reflection practice: "Stop the glorification of busy," and "Don't just do something, sit there."

What is your number one obstacle preventing you from meditating?

What do the quotes mean to you?

How do you glorify busyness?

Do you notice others glorifying busyness?

When and where in your life are you doing something when you should be sitting there?

WEEK EIGHTEEN

Real Questions about Meditation #2

These questions come from a group of legal professionals at a large law firm, as well as from attendees of a monthly meditation gathering at a yoga studio.

Q) Am I supposed to be present and focused the entire time?
A) Yes and no. The idea is that we work toward being more present for *more* of the time in our meditation sessions, as well as in life. By being more present in our sessions we develop the parts of the brain (such as the thalamus, insula, anterior cingulate cortex, and parts of the prefrontal cortex)[28] that help us stay present in other areas of our life. The consequences for going through your day on auto-pilot range from mild to severe. Every summer you hear stories about parents forgetting that they left their infant or young child in the car while they went to work, only to realize the terrible truth after it's too late. More common though, is that we go through our days never really being present and alert to what is happening in the here and now. We miss out on the only part of life that is real — not memory or fantasy — the present moment.

However, we can't expect to be present for the entire duration of our meditation every day and time. Remember that the human mind is effectively designed to daydream. We're working against the evolution of the human brain when we sit in meditation, so be patient and forgiving when the mind drifts.

Q) What should I do when I catch myself daydreaming?
A) Gently bring it back without judgment. When you catch yourself daydreaming, you can take a moment to notice what you're thinking about, noting whether the emotion that goes with the thought is positive, negative, or neutral, and noting where in the body that emotion manifests itself. Avoid turning your meditation into a struggle. Let your attention to the present be a soft hold, not a white-knuckle grip.

Q) Do I need to meditate every day to get the benefits?
A) No. You can start to feel less stressed and more calm even if you only meditate once, but as with most things, the more you meditate the faster you'll start to feel the positive results. Most studies are based on twenty minutes every day for eight weeks. But some studies found results just after one twenty-minute session!

What are some of the problems you've encountered in your life by not being present?

How do you think practicing meditation can help you?

If you could ask any question about your meditation practice what would it be?

Section 3
WEEKS NINETEEN THROUGH TWENTY-SIX

Mindfulness for Work

WEEK NINETEEN

Do it for the Team!
Meditation in the Workplace

Some people like to meditate first thing in the morning; others, right before bed. But there are good reasons for also bringing your meditation practice to your work place. If the idea of stopping your work, closing your office door, and sitting quietly for ten minutes seems inappropriate, it might help for you to think of your meditation practice as an act dedicated to being a better team player.

Consider this question. Who's the better team player: the co-worker who skips lunch every day to keep working or the one who takes a few breaks throughout the day? If you picked the latter, you're right. Research from the University of Illinois Urbana-Champaign shows that people who take short and frequent breaks are better able to focus on their tasks by avoiding attention fatigue.[29] When people are counting on you to get work done, taking breaks ensures you're delivering your best product.

If taking a break from work is good, taking a break for meditation is even better. According to several studies, including one by a team of psychologists at University Santa Barbara, meditation improves working memory.[30] Working memory is the system by which people store information they need "at the ready" — for decision-making and reasoning. Meditation is also linked with improved executive functioning, defined as self and resource management in pursuit of a task. Meditation sharpens the skills of emotional acceptance and self-monitoring that are part of self-management.[31]

Meditation, then, will help you work smarter, and that's something your colleagues will appreciate.

Consider how taking care of yourself is good for your team at work or on the home front. How do you build self-care into your daily routine?

What are some ways that you can take a smart break from your work?

WEEK TWENTY

Better Decision-Making

Did you know that numerous large corporations have in-house meditation programs for employees? Companies such as Apple, Google, AOL Time Warner, General Mills, Green Mountain Coffee, Nike, and Under Armour are just a smattering of reported companies that offer workplace meditation. There are many good reasons for these companies to invest money and sanction work breaks. Those ten to twenty minutes of meditation not only improve your working memory and executive function, they also make you a better decision-maker.

In one highly-referenced study, conducted by INSEAD and the Wharton School of Business, researchers found that meditation (even just one 15-minute session) improved decision-making skills.[32] The researchers found that meditators were less likely than their non-meditating peers to succumb to what is called "sunk cost bias" — the tendency for people to "throw good money (time/effort/energy) after bad." For example, a team might decide to invest in developing a new product only to suspect after considerable time and financial investment that the product is a bust. People who practice mindfulness meditation are better able, than people who don't, to have the clarity to back out of a bad plan, no matter how many resources have already been invested in it.

The authors speculate that the ability of mindfulness to improve our mood and draw our attention to the present moment improves our decision-making skills.

Another smaller study found that students who meditate were also much less emotionally reactive to perceived "unfairness" than their non-meditating peers.[33] Organizations and workplace teams need people who bring rationality and self-awareness to the table. When you practice mindfulness meditation you are helping your organization avoid falling for a common decision-making fallacy. Meditation makes you a great asset on any team.

Is there a long-standing commitment in your work or personal life which you maintain in spite of the cost outweighing the benefits?

Can you reflect on that commitment this week? How can better decision-making skills help you?

WEEK TWENTY-ONE

Happiness and Productivity

Another reason companies are willing to invest in meditation practice is that it makes people happier, and happier people are more productive employees.[34]

Over the past two weeks, we've seen how meditation improves working memory, focus, and decision-making skills. The most impressive research on meditation, however, addresses the connection between the practice and happiness. After decades of meditating, the man dubbed the "happiest man in the world," Matthieu Ricard (a former molecular PhD scientist turned Buddhist monk), has been found to have extraordinary high and fMRI-measurable levels of upbeat brain activity and nearly invisible levels of negative activity.[35] Ricard promotes the idea that happiness is a decision you make through a disciplined practice rather than the outcome of events or circumstances in your life.

Numerous studies have found that meditation has a therapeutic impact on anxiety and depression. In fact, Mindfulness-Based Cognitive Therapy and Dialectical Behavior Therapy, used to treat mental and mood disorders, have large components of mindfulness awareness in their makeup. Learning to quiet the mind, in effect, helps people recognize when they are being besieged by repetitive and non-productive worrisome thoughts and then gives them the tools to engage in more realistic and helpful thinking.

According to what scientists calls the Yerkes-Dodson Law, some degree of stress and anxiety actually increases productivity, up to a point.[36] When stress levels become too high, productivity diminishes.

If you're a manager, one take-away here is that you need to manage stress levels: keep your direct reports on a deadline with clear expectations, but make sure the deadline and expectations are realistic. A high-stakes team, in particular, needs to guard against the threat of too much stress or productivity will be adversely affected. Another take-away: bring mindfulness into the workplace to help employees lower their stress levels.

Do you have a tendency to be more stressed than your peers over work projects, or less?

What does it mean to you to view happiness as a choice rather than as a by-product of life circumstances?

Would your life look any different if you saw happiness as a choice?

WEEK TWENTY-TWO

Health and Productivity

One theme of mindfulness for work is that the way to be the best employee or colleague is to be your best self—smart, focused, happy, and healthy. We've covered smart, focused, and happy; this week we're looking at healthy.

Research on mindfulness notes numerous health benefits with regard to eating, sleeping, and reducing physical ailments. Mindful eating (see December: Mindful Eating for the Holidays) increases our tendency to eat more healthfully by reducing the likelihood of over-eating, stress-eating, and making poor food choices. When we take the time to actually enjoy and notice the experience of eating, we become more attuned to the sensation of fullness. We are also less likely to find ourselves mindlessly standing in front of the freezer eating ice cream out of the carton at 11:00 PM because of stress.

Mindfulness has also been linked to better sleep. According to the American Sleep Association, roughly 60 million Americans suffer from sleep disorders, including insomnia and sleep apnea.[37] In one JAMA article, researchers reported that mindfulness meditation significantly improved the quality of sleep and daytime performance for people suffering from moderate but chronic sleep disturbances.[38] See Week Thirty-Five for more detailed information on mindfulness and sleep.

Some other mindfulness benefits being explored by medical researchers are lowered blood pressure (probably because of lower levels of stress),[39] and reduction in inflammation on a cellular level which can reduce cancer risks.[40] Finally, mindfulness practice has been found to be a powerful tool for managing chronic pain instead of using addicting opioids.[41]

The research on meditation and health is ongoing. For updates, go to the online catalog of professional health publications (https://

www.ncbi.nlm.nih.gov/pubmed) and type in "mindfulness" to see the array of the most recent, peer-reviewed research on the physical and psychological benefits of mindfulness.

Which foundation of physical health do you want to work on the most: healthy eating, exercise, or sleep?

How would an improvement in your health benefit your career and other parts of your life?

If you manage people or an office, how would having healthier employees improve your workplace environment?

WEEK TWENTY-THREE

Managing Crunch Times

Every workplace and industry has regular seasons when work becomes overloaded. For CPAs, for example, it's late March and April. For physicians at a teaching hospital, it's July when the new residents arrive, and for professors, it's end-of-semester grading in December and May. Some work environments have less predictable crunch times, but big, high-stakes projects will always come along to spike stress levels.

Whether it's a regularly scheduled crunch time or a special occasion form of crunch, follow these mindfulness-based guidelines to make even the most intense moments a little less painful.

Return to the present moment experience when tensions start running high. Stress is often based on the fear of not meeting future deadlines. By returning the mind to the present, we can lower stress.

Be aware of the levels of stress you are under and be kind and compassionate to yourself. Practice *metta* meditation. (See Week Seven.)

Same goes for how you treat your co-workers.

Find a conscious breath pattern, such as *ujjayi* or three-part exhalation. (See Week Forty-Eight.)

Become aware of and mindfully release any tension you are holding in your body, especially in the hands, belly, shoulders, neck, jaw, and brows.

Stress sometimes arises when you want the present moment to be other than it is. Find a degree of surrender in or acceptance of the current circumstances.

Remember that this stressful season or project has an end date, even if you don't know when it is. (You might even miss the excitement when you're done!)

While you are in crunch time, what can you delegate or completely let go of?

How does practicing compassion to yourself and others help with workplace stress?

Can it also help with how you manage workplace stress on the home front?

Use the quietness of mindfulness meditation to create the space in which the answers to these questions can arise.

A Moment of Mindfulness Before a Meeting

When we're meditating, our minds will often start to wander. They might go off on a stream of consciousness for several minutes before we catch ourselves and bring them back. Often, we think of the mind wandering as a failure, and yet, in fact, the real success is not in keeping the mind from wandering but in the bringing it back and beginning again.

One of the most profound lessons meditation teaches us is that we can always, always, always begin again. Any moment is a time to begin again. No matter how far down the wrong path we've gone, we can turn around. We already saw how this (begin again) mindset plays out in terms of rational decision-making and "sunk cost bias" (Week Twenty).

Another benefit of meditation's "begin again" approach for the workplace comes as people move from one task or challenge to another. Do you really want Fred's frustration with his computer crashing, or Elaine's upset over a lost client to be the backdrop for your meeting on increasing inbound sales and marketing? Wouldn't you prefer that people approach your meeting with a fresh and present-minded perspective? The answer is an obvious "yes."

The next time you're running a meeting, try starting it with one minute of silence, focusing on breath and perhaps asking attendees to visualize setting aside their thoughts, concerns, and emotions which are unrelated to the current meeting. I had one client who visualized carrying her "gremlins" out of the conference room and telling them to "sit down and don't move" until she came out to retrieve them. The benefit is that the attendees will have an opportunity to "begin again" — letting go of whatever just happened in their day (a rough morning commute, an IT frustration, a distracting email) prior to arriving at the meeting. Offer your team a chance to hit the "reset" button with a minute of mindful breathing, and then they'll approach

the work at hand feeling mentally refreshed.

Spend a minute before you arrive at your next meeting, or before picking up the phone to call someone, with a minute of silence and reflect on how differently you feel during the meeting or while on the call.

Mindfulness and Interpersonal Relations

You haven't come this far in life without more than once being told that you cannot control other people; you can only control yourself and your reactions to others. And yet, still, the temptation to change others (often in the guise of helping them) is hard to resist.

In one company where I consulted on mindfulness, I was, from time to time, asked to "get" certain people in the office to attend the mindfulness sessions. I was told that "John" or "Susan" really needed mindfulness. They were really stressed. They really needed to relax and let go. And they probably did, but often the very people who recommended others for the sessions were not showing up either.

Mindfulness works both ways. It not only makes you calmer and happier, but it also helps you deal better with other people who are not calm or happy.

When you find yourself feeling resentful, out of control, and distraught, or you find yourself in frequent angry exchanges with people you work or live with, then you owe yourself and others some time during the week for meditation practice. Think of your own emotional state and your interactions with coworkers like a meat thermometer: a read on your inner life.

It's tempting to attribute your emotions and reactions to the actions of others, but when it comes down to it, if someone is bothering you, mindfulness will help you manage your response. If a colleague is crazy stressed and lashing out, your mindfulness practice can help buffer the negative effects.

Who should be practicing mindfulness? If you think it's the other person, it's probably you, too.

What can you do for yourself to make you happier and more pleasant at work and at home?

How does it feel to have mindfulness as part of your regular routine?

What changes in your life do you notice from your practice?

Morning Resolve for Workplace Success

Later in the book (see Week Thirty-Three), we'll take a look at a morning resolve created by Mahatma Gandhi, the world-famous promoter of peaceful activism and Indian independence. Many meditators like to begin their day by reciting or chanting a resolve or intention for their inner life. This intention can be said out loud or silently before or after sitting in silence. Setting an intention gives you a sense of purpose and perspective for the day. It also helps you to remember and reinforce your priorities and values. This week offers a suggestion for setting intentions around workplace success:

May I be humble.

May I have relationships at work that are positive and inspiring.

May I seek and find activities and goals that inspire me and tap into my strengths and passions.

May I confront my greatest challenges with determination and grounded self-assurance.

May I use my time wisely and with conscious intent.

May I stay committed to personal growth with hopefulness and humility.

May I remember that I am more than just my position and title at work.

May I remember the people at home and at work
who depend on me.

May I have balance between taking care of others
and taking care of myself.

*Which of the resolve statements speaks to you most at
this time?*

What would or did you add to this resolve?

*Do certain of these resolves speak to you more deeply over-
all, or does the significance of them vary from day to day?*

*How can you bring these intentions to the top of your
consciousness throughout the day?*

Section 4

Reflections for Personal Development

WEEK TWENTY-SEVEN

Gratitude — Replacing Suffering with Joy

The sages define suffering as wanting things to be different than they are.

The experience of gratitude, however, renders the complete opposite effect. When we cultivate a feeling of appreciation, we feel happy, maybe even blessed. Gratitude requires a mindful attention to what is good in your life. When we're not mindful, we are likely to give all of our attention to the squeaky wheel while losing perspective for the well-oiled ones.

Research on gratitude suggests that we can even transform our suffering into joy through the act of feeling and expressing thanks. People who report more gratitude in their life also report better emotional, mental and physical health. A number of studies have found evidence for the logical idea that couples who express gratitude towards each other are happier together and have a stronger relationship.[42] Other studies have linked improved sleep[43] and more frequent exercise and other self-care practices as positive outcomes of gratitude.[44]

Having a mindful and robust gratitude practice can involve keeping a gratitude journal, making sure you say thanks at every possible moment (when strangers hold doors for you, when a friend does you a small favor...), creating gratitude rituals around meals, bedtime, waking up, or other typical moments of the day, or taking complaint sabbaths (days without a single complaint).

This week, replace suffering with joy. The moment you find yourself wishing life could be different, find something which makes you feel grateful (no matter how small). Even more powerful, take the very thing you wish were different, and find something about it that you can appreciate.

In addition, spend a few moments in your meditation practice this week finding something for which you can be grateful for in that moment (while you are meditating).

Spend a minute finding and cultivating a sense of gratitude for something in your present-moment experience — your health, employment, family, loved-ones, and material comforts such as heat in the winter and air-conditioning in the summer.

Then spend a minute seeking gratitude for something in your past which was tough to live through or manage but which you can now see provided you with inner strength, confidence, appreciation, a sense of purpose, or some other gift.

WEEK TWENTY-EIGHT

Practicing Non-Judgment

The world would be a better place if, more frequently, we just gave each other a break.

Better than anyone else, Eckhardt Tolle, in *A New Earth*, explains the connection between judgment and the ego. He notes that criticism and complaint are ways that we try to make ourselves feel better about ourselves. By finding fault in the other, we plant a stake in the ground that says, "I am not that!" By calling someone else, say, an idiot, we are essentially saying, "I'm smart enough to know that you are stupid."[45]

Notice in traffic, how angry people can become when someone makes an error. The truth is that none of us are perfect drivers. We've all made mistakes while driving, but when others do, we often react as if our own driving is an unblemished record of attention, care, and skill.

How can we become less judgmental of others? Here's where things get interesting. We can start by cutting ourselves a break—treating ourselves with compassion and kindness rather than harsh criticism and unreasonable demands. Sometimes we should listen to how harsh our inner dialogue is with ourselves. Listen to yourself the next time you make a mistake such as losing a credit card, leaving something important at home, forgetting to set your alarm, or missing a work deadline.

Remember that Jon Kabat-Zinn defines mindfulness as the purposeful paying attention to the present moment, *non-judgmentally*. In our meditation practice, each time we bring our mind back to the present moment without judgment we are training ourselves to be kinder and more compassionate, first to ourselves and then to others.

Notice this week how judgment of yourself and others plays out in your day-to-day life.

Are there particular conditions or situations where your critical self is most active?

True, Kind, Necessary

Is it True? Is it Kind? Is it Necessary?

One of the benefits of mindfulness is, to paraphrase Viktor Frankl, the space it creates between stimulus and response. In that space between, we find choice. Mindfulness then creates time for us to choose our response. (Over time, the practice of making that choice helps us to create new neural pathways, which then become our new default responses.) One such choice is the words we use, or more generally, what we give voice to.

There is an ethic within the mindfulness community that our inclination to speak should be filtered through three sieves. First, is what you are about to say true? Is it true, both superficially and viscerally? For example, if a colleague asks you for help, and you are not feeling inclined to give up your time to help, how do you respond from a place of truth? Do you say, "I would love to help you but I have a previous commitment?" No, because you would not "love" to help, nor do you have a previous commitment. Instead, you could say, "I have been extremely busy lately and am running myself ragged. I promised myself that I would get home from work at a reasonable hour tonight. Is there another time I can help you?"

Second, is what you are about to say kind? Does it come from your heart with compassion and a sense of warmth and connection, or is it a reflection of your ego and emanating from a place of hurt, anger, or just carelessness? If you hear two other co-workers sharing gossip about another person in your office, do you join in, or do you excuse yourself from the conversation? Likewise, if a child or someone who reports to you comes to you and admits that they made a mistake, can you be firm while staying kind in your response, or does your ego need to humiliate and put them down?

Finally, are the words you are about to utter necessary? Some of us fill up our lives with unnecessary chatter when often silence is what we and others need. When I return every year from my week at a silent meditation retreat, I notice that I am much less inclined to engage in chit-chat. I appreciate the quiet and only engage in conversation when necessary. I try to let my sense of peacefulness and ease speak for me instead of relying on words.

When mindfulness practice allows you to fully consider what and when to speak, you create a more truthful, kinder, and more meaningful world.

Can you notice your words this week and pay special attention to whether they are true, kind and necessary?

WEEK THIRTY

Finding Peace

Over twelve years ago, I bought a refrigerator magnet about finding peace. I knew very keenly that the people I loved the most needed me to be calmer in my heart. The quote on the magnet challenged my inherent belief that I would only find peace when my kids were both in school all day, the house was cleaner, my job was better, my extended family stopped being so annoying, I finished writing my first book and got it published, and the stars aligned perfectly. The refrigerator magnet helped me see that equanimity is an inside job, independent of external circumstances.

So, I bought the magnet and put it on my refrigerator to remind myself to be more peaceful. My next lesson turned out to be that reminding yourself to be peaceful when you go to get eggs out of the fridge isn't enough. You need to commit to a regular practice that cultivates a calm mind and heart.

If you'd like to be less reactive and you're stuck thinking it'll only happen when the stars align in just the right order, it's time to hold yourself responsible for finding equanimity.

Meditation is not just about reducing stress, but, perhaps more importantly, it helps us cultivate an inner stillness which protects us from the surrounding chaos. That's why in meditation you sit in complete stillness. You might feel sensations arise like an itch on your neck or an ache in your big toe, but you learn to notice those stimuli but not react to them. It takes practice and eventually over time, we have calmness in our heart.

If finding more peace in your life sounds appealing, recommit to your meditation practice.

Peace—It does not mean to be in a place where there is no noise, trouble or hard work. It means to be in the midst of those things and still be calm in your heart. (Unkonwn)

How important is having more peace in your life?

How much time during your day are you willing to devote to feeling more peaceful?

WEEK THIRTY-ONE

Meditation is Not a Selfish Practice

Sometimes, investing time sitting quietly, can be perceived as self-indulgent naval-gazing. Here I present nine reasons why mindfulness is the best thing you can do to help others.

One: Meditation helps slow down your reactivity between stimulus and response, thus enabling you to carefully choose your response to, say, critical comments or back-talking teenagers.

Two: Self-compassion leads to compassion for others. We cannot give to others what we don't know how to give to ourselves.

Three: Mindful awareness of our emotions increases our emotional intelligence, allowing us to connect more appropriately to others' needs and challenges.

Four: Mindfulness teaches you to pay attention to the present moment and helps to alleviate the unnecessary anxiety we feel about the future and the similarly unnecessary remorse or guilt we may feel about the past.

Five: Meditation teaches us to pay attention to details in the present moment, which we might otherwise miss. For example, when we are driving, we will notice that the pedestrian crossing in front of us is distracted by his phone and we will be more careful before we proceed through the light.

Six: Meditation teaches us to stay calm under duress. This calmness might be lifesaving in moments of crisis as we choose the correct course of action to take.

Seven: Mindfulness helps us be more aware of how much our ego converts everything to its own use. Even our attempts at humility can devolve into food for the ego (i.e. "I'm the most humble person here"). With awareness, we can keep the ego in check.

Eight: People who meditate report being happier than people who don't, and happiness through mindfulness (as opposed to happiness by buying more things or controlling others) is good for society.

Nine: Taking time out of your day to pay attention to yourself can be the best thing you can do for others. It's not selfish to eat healthy food or get exercise. Neither is it selfish to take ten to thirty minutes to sit quietly and become aware of your thoughts.

Ultimately, the work you do in mindfulness is about being a better, kinder, more compassionate and caring you. That's the you the world needs in order to be a more peaceful place. There's nothing selfish about that.

For whom are you practicing mediation?

What benefits in your life and in the lives of others do you hope to achieve through your meditation?

Do you give yourself permission to be quiet and still before you begin practice?

WEEK THIRTY-TWO

Finding Deep Relaxation:
The Physical Body in Meditation

How your body aligns in meditation is important, whether you are sitting on the floor or in a chair. It's essential to feel a firm connection with the floor (either through the "sit bones" — the lower portion of the pelvis — or through the feet). It's also always appropriate to keep the spine long.

The longer we pay attention to relaxing the muscles the more we realize how much tension we are holding in them out of habit. For example, when we sit in chairs, many of us tend to tuck our feet in, which means our leg muscles are engaged. Instead, walk your feet out so that your ankles are directly under your knees. For the purposes of meditation, keep your legs uncrossed and notice if you are unconsciously engaging (squeezing) your thigh muscles. Make sure, instead, that they relax and spiral out. Finally, allow your belly to be soft and your hands to relax at your side or in your lap, rather than crossing your arms on your chest or interlocking your fingers.

Begin your meditation paying attention to the most obvious places you hold tension in the muscles — often it's in the hands, neck and jaw, or shoulders. Soften those muscles first, and then return your attention to those locations again, while also starting to pay attention to the other areas where you might be holding in tension (say, between the eyebrows — I frequently see people holding tension there).

I have found that I can spend an entire meditation just focusing on releasing tension in my facial muscles. Interestingly, one of the Hebrew phrases for endless patience or equanimity (*arich anpin*) translates directly to "long face." One of the outcomes of meditation is a feeling of lengthening the muscles in our bodies by releasing them. The more you release the holding patterns in your muscles the more relaxed you'll feel.

Which parts of the body are the obvious places where you hold in tension?

As you sit longer in stillness, what are some of the other places of tension you discover?

WEEK THIRTY-THREE

Gandhi's Morning Resolution

Morning Resolutions (spoken like a mantra) like the one introduced in Week Twenty-Six are a great way to begin or complete your daily meditation. A morning resolution sets your intention for the day and brings it to the forefront of your mind, thus reinforcing your most deeply held values.

Gandhi suggested that "the first act of every morning be a resolve such as this:

I shall not fear anyone on Earth.

I shall fear only God.

I shall not bear ill will toward anyone.

I shall not submit to injustice from anyone.

I shall conquer untruth by truth. And in resisting untruth, I shall put up with all suffering."

This week you can create your own morning resolution focused on the big picture of who you are and what you stand for, as Gandhi did with his. Consider what your most important values are and how you want to orient yourself in this world. In other words, choose resolves that focus on big ideas. "I shall treat my body with utmost respect" is a higher level of resolve than "I shall not eat dessert today." Keep it short. Gandhi's is only five lines and 45 words. Repeat your resolution before or after you meditate and throughout your day to keep yourself on target.

It's interesting to note that the morning resolution written by Gandhi begins with the words "I shall." Your morning resolution can start with other declarations such as "May I" or "I will." Pick language that is powerful and meaningful to you.

What part of Gandhi's resolution speaks most fully to you this week? Why?

What core values do you want to affirm every morning in order to align your actions and intentions for the rest of the day?

Can you write your own morning resolution for this week?

Mindfulness and Emotional Intelligence

In essential terms, emotional intelligence is the ability to recognize emotions in yourself and others and to regulate your own. Mindfulness and emotional Intelligence (EI) are highly linked. In fact, one study suggests that mindfulness's positive impact on a person's well-being is mediated through increased EI.[46] The ability to step out of our experience of an emotion (anger, sadness, fear, happiness) to name and observe it is at the heart of EI and one of the four foundations of mindfulness meditation.

When we meditate, we keep observing all that is happening in the present moment, including our thoughts and emotions. Take a moment to identify the emotion you're feeling the next time you sit down at your desk.

Psychologists are not in complete agreement about how many emotions there are, or even which are the core emotions. The chart on the opposite page is a good place to start to build your sense of your core emotions and to more readily label your feelings. Practice identifying your emotions when you are not meditating and then when your eyes are closed in meditation, the categories will be easy to recall. After a bit of practice, the categories will feel intuitive.

The second step is then to identify where in the body you are experiencing that emotion: your chest, jaw, throat, belly, or somewhere else. When you are angry you might notice how the feeling manifests in your jaw or throat. Likewise, when you are nervous, the feeling may be felt in the abdomen (the GI system, i.e. "butterflies in your stomach"). The more we dig into our emotional experiences, the more "intelligence" we gather, and thereby increase our understanding of our inner emotional life.

PEACEFUL	HAPPY	ANGRY	SAD	AFRAID	SHAME/GUILT
content	joyous	seething	disappointed	fearful	embarrassed
satisfied	pleased	offended	depressed	nervous	ashamed
calm	grateful	frustrated	grieving	stressed	self-conscious
relaxed	playful	angry	discouraged	overwhelmed	regretful
mellow	hopeful	impatient	pessimistic	worried	humiliated
serene	amused	annoyed	anguished	anxious	guilty

In which category of emotion do you most frequently find yourself when you check-in?

How challenging is it for you to identify the more subtle expressions of a particular emotion?

Are there any emotions which feel embarrassing for you to admit to feeling?

Going a little deeper, do you bring judgment to certain emotions as being okay or not okay, or right vs. wrong?

WEEK THIRTY-FIVE

Meditation and Sleep

We live in an era of profound deprivation. We have traded away one of our most important resources for health and happiness in return for material goods and status. I'm talking about sleep, and though you simply might resolve to get more sleep tonight, it's not always that easy. While a lot of us choose to get less sleep, many more simply cannot get the sleep they need because of insomnia (difficulty falling or staying asleep). Over 50% of Americans report trouble with sleep at least a few nights per week.[47] Around 30% of people have trouble with sleep on a daily basis.

A groundbreaking study in 2015 found meditation to be a highly effective remedy for people with significant sleep problems.[48] Experts speculate that meditating for twenty minutes during the day trains the mind and body to relax, and that training becomes important when it's time to go to bed in the evening. In addition, mindfulness teaches the mind how to let go of thinking, which helps people let go of their thoughts (about work or other stresses in their life) much more easily when it's time to go to bed, or when they wake up in the middle of the night.

The counting-the-breath method of meditation (see Week Three) is an especially helpful tool for clearing the mind of thinking when you are trying to get sleep.

Here are some other tips to help you get a better night of rest. Stay away from all screens (including the television) for at least an hour before bed. Keep yourself on a regular daily sleep/wake schedule. Avoid caffeine, dark chocolate and other stimulating foods in the evenings.

What can you do to create a going-to-bed routine that will signal to your mind and body that you are ready to settle down for the night?

WEEK THIRTY-SIX

Journaling

Do you journal?

Meditation and journaling can work together like bookends on your day. By recording your thoughts, you give them more attention and take the opportunity for reflection. Another way to think about journaling is that it empties the brain of the thoughts you have carried around all day so that when you meditate in the morning, your mind is less busy. And mindfulness helps with journaling by generating more clarity in your thoughts, rendering them easier to get down on paper.

Here are some tips for adding a journaling practice to your routine:

Begin your day with ten or more minutes of meditation, and finish your day with a few minutes of journaling.

All you need to journal is a notebook, a pen, and a few minutes to contemplate and write at the end of the day. You might find it helpful to leave the notebook and pen on your bedside table.

When you write, don't worry about grammar, spelling, or punctuation. You're not writing for an audience other than yourself. You're not writing an autobiography or something you intend to be published.

As you journal, take five to ten minutes to check in with your thoughts and emotions. You don't have to write a lot. Just invest a few minutes of time before bed to review your day and current feelings. Thoughts and emotions that we are aware of cannot sneak up and overwhelm us. Taking a few minutes every day to get in touch with our feelings is a great mental health practice.

What do you think of when you think about keeping a journal?

How do you think journaling will be helpful to you?

Can you find a journaling partner to help keep you accountable?

WEEK THIRTY-SEVEN

Active Listening

Listening is a very poorly understood, yet vital component of good communication. Most of us would agree that when we are speaking, we aim to be heard and understood. Yet, quite often when we are listening to others, we are usually listening to respond or rebut. The gap between how we want others to hear us and how we listen to others can be bridged when we engage in active listening. Active listening is listening to validate and understand the other person, as opposed to the listening we typically do, which engages our minds in efforts to either counter or take over the conversation.

Active listening is a skill which benefits every aspect of your life: in family life with partners and children, at work with colleagues, managers, and customers, and in public life, interacting with people as we go about our day. It allows you to engage with others in a more productive way. When you listen to understand rather than to argue back, you can hear crucial information you might miss otherwise.

You can hone your ability to focus by paying attention to the inner thoughts that arise during meditation. When your mind wanders during meditation, notice the thoughts that draw your attention. Where does the mind keep wandering to? Don't judge yourself for either letting the mind wander or for the content of the thoughts. Also, acknowledge the emotions associated with those thoughts before returning your awareness to your breath.

The pillars of mindfulness are the same as active listening. Be curious. Let go of judgment. Ask questions. Seek understanding.

Where can you bring active listening into your life for better relationships?

What did you notice after bringing active listening into a conversation with someone?

What did you hear that you might not have heard otherwise?

Do you know anyone who is a very good listener? What makes him or her good at listening?

WEEK THIRTY-EIGHT

Mindfulness Meditation and Creativity

Creativity is the ability to make connections between two or more things in a unique manner. For many people, creative expression is one of the joys of life, and for others it is also part of their livelihood. A certain line in a poem or song lyric, or a color used in a painting can enhance our experience of life and allow us to see the world in a new way. Creativity, as the midwife of invention, also leads us to new solutions for old problems, such as the weave of an undershirt that wicks away sweat during vigorous exercise, or a way to operate on people using the smallest incisions possible, thereby shortening their recovery time.

There is a persistent myth that people are either born creative or they're not. To some degree, creativity does seem to be a matter of genetics. And yet, research also suggests that certain brain patterns, which are conducive to fostering creativity, can be enhanced. Scientists have noted that long-term practitioners of mindfulness meditation show higher levels of creativity than their non-meditating peers.[49] In particular, the Open Monitoring (OM) method of meditation, in which the practitioner simply pays attention to whatever thought or sensation arises in the present moment, without judgment, increases scores on Alternate Use Tests (AUTs). (AUTs ask participants to list out as many uses as they can imagine for common household items such as a paperclip or a piece of string.) In a series of studies on OM meditation and creativity, the skill of observation was found to "not only [have] improved working memory, it also increased cognitive flexibility and reduced cognitive rigidity—all of which are critical to the creative process."[50]

Steve Jobs was a longtime practitioner of Zen meditation as a means of priming his creativity levels (as well as reducing stress and clearing his mind). He sought out teachers on the West Coast and even traveled to India to bolster his practice. Many observers have drawn a direct connection between Jobs' meditation practice (a refining of the technology of the brain) and his ability to refine the technology of personal computing. Even the emphasis on simplicity in design can be traced to the Zen philosophy behind Jobs' embrace of Zen meditation.

What activities in your life are outlets for creative expression?

What types of creative solutions do you need most in your life right now?

WEEK THIRTY-NINE

Cultivating Humility Through Mindfulness

Evidence of the importance of humility is all around us, from the myth of Icarus who flew too close to the sun to the modern news stories of people in powerful places brought down by arrogance. Confucius said that "humility is the foundation of all virtues." But what does it mean to have humility? Quite simply, it is the proper assessment of who we truly are. It's the balance point between self-effacement and arrogance, between under or over-valuing our abilities and skills. Humility is also the proper apportionment of your time and energy as directed to yourself and others.

Humility is central to virtue because it allows us to learn and grow. Through humility we can admit when we are going down the wrong path and then turn ourselves around.

Mindfulness and meditation are integral to humility in several respects. One, meditation is not easy. When we find our minds wandering we must be aware of the wandering and then humbly turn ourselves around and return back to the present. And we must do this repeatedly... again and again. Two, mindfulness enables us to assess who we are in regard to our strengths and weaknesses. It informs us about the truth of who we really are, not who we believe we are or wish to be. Three, mindfulness allows us to see how, as Eckhardt Tolle says in his best selling book, *A New Earth*, the ego converts everything for its own use. Only when we are fully present can we avoid making everything about ourselves, such as taking an act of philanthropy and making it about how generous and kind we are.

Thus, we can see how mindfulness helps strengthen our path toward a life of humility and general virtue.

How balanced are you in your understanding of your strengths and weaknesses?

How do you think that mindfulness could play a role in making you (even) more balanced in your sense of humility?

The Reality of Certainty and Control

Let your practice be a refuge from your need to control.
Rolf Gates

As I write, an early spring snowstorm is bearing down on the mid-Atlantic area. Once again, everyone is bracing for impact, wondering how much accumulation there will be and if our weekend plans will be left intact or need to be rescheduled. Natural disasters like hurricanes, floods, and earthquakes remind us that we humans, arguably the smartest creatures on our planet, have limited control and unlimited uncertainty. We might be able to choose where we live; we can choose how we prepare in advance of danger or whether we want to evacuate. We can reuse and recycle more, and drive a Prius in order to reduce our carbon footprint and our effect on global warming, but in the face of an actual force of nature, our relative power is insignificant. We cannot control and we cannot fully predict.

Mindfulness meditation heightens our self-awareness, which helps us with our ability to discern both when we have power and when we do not, and then either guide our actions or make peace with our powerlessness and the resultant uncertainty.

When we sit in stillness, we allow ourselves to observe what is without needing to change anything in that moment. Loud sounds come and go. The need to cough or scratch an itch arises and then retreats. We can just sit and watch sensations and needs come and go without reacting to them. In this way we train our minds to be more comfortable with letting go of control. Making peace with our occasional powerlessness and uncertainty saves us from unnecessary suffering.

This week, can you bring greater attention to moments when you want control or certainty, both while you're meditating and when you're not?

Do you notice any patterns around your desire for greater control and certainty — under what circumstances does it arise?

How does it feel to let go of your need to control or be certain when you are meditating?

Section 5

Deepest Reflections

Everything is Temporary

Some say the whole of human experience can be summarized as trying to hold on to what is pleasurable and to avoid what is unpleasant. But both responses of grasping and rejecting cause us pain because everything—the pleasure, the pain and all things between—is temporary.

For example, if you had a lovely holiday week and you were trying to hold onto that loveliness, you now find yourself on Monday morning feeling sad or frustrated that the time was so short (so temporary). Likewise, if you had a rude house guest for a few days and you spent the whole visit feeling frustrated that he or she wasn't nicer, then you made yourself miserable because you lost sight that they would soon be leaving.

How differently do you experience life when you recognize that nothing is permanent? People change, jobs change, relationships wax and wane, children grow up, parents get older, presidents come and go, even the biggest of buildings go up and eventually are razed for newer buildings.

This past weekend, I spent some time walking around the neighborhood where I grew up. I made a point to walk down streets I don't usually visit, and I even walked around the elementary school building I attended from kindergarten through second grade. The walk made me keenly aware of two things: impermanence and attachment. I realized how much I missed the people and experiences from my childhood and became acutely aware of my desire to grasp and hold on to places and people long gone from my life. I was filled with a sense of loss and the struggle to hold on. I just kept walking and observed the feelings and thoughts arise and then dissipate.

The awareness of my feelings helped minimize my own suffering. What happens when we are not aware? Though ignorance can sometimes equal bliss, more often it leads to suffering. Being mindful of our present moment experience means that our thoughts, feelings, and needs don't sneak up on us in unhealthy ways. We get to process them in real time and with compassion and wisdom.

Mindfulness allows you to see the temporary nature of your thoughts and feelings and the uselessness of grasping and resisting. Instead, we come to peace with what is, knowing that it is, for better or worse, temporary.

What can you recognize about your life right now as not permanent?

What are you trying to hold on to?

What are you trying to push away?

WEEK FORTY-TWO

The Power of Non-Thinking: Athletes and Getting into the Zone

When I was first exposed to the idea of non-thinking, I deeply resisted the concept. To my way of thinking (irony noted), there was no problem which couldn't be solved by thinking—the more thinking, the more solution. The idea that thinking can be the antithesis to success isn't just an idea promoted by meditation gurus dressed in robes. It has allies and subscribers from surprisingly different backgrounds. Sports coaches, in particular, recognize that peak performance relies on the suppression of the thinking/analyzing mind.

Not too long ago, I was discussing "the zone" with a prominent Mid-Atlantic golf-coach. The zone refers to the state of mind when the pre-frontal context is disengaged and sports performance peaks. The coach explained that he employs many tricks to move his athletes away from the thinking mind and into the experiential mind (what mindfulness meditators call "the present moment").

Likewise, *The Inner Game of Tennis: The Classic Guide to the Mental Side of Peak Performance* by W. Timothy Gallwey does a great job in laying bare the benefits of being in the moment rather than in the thinking mind. Gallwey observed that, "When a tennis player is 'in the zone,' he's not thinking about how, when or even where to hit the ball. He's not trying to hit the ball, and after the shot he doesn't think about how badly or how well he made contact. The ball seems to get hit through a process which doesn't require thought. There may be an awareness of the sight, sound and feel of the ball, and even of the tactical situation, but the player just seems to know what to do without thinking about it."

He identifies the three most important "inner skills" for peak performance:

Non-judgmental awareness

Visualization of success

Trust (a letting-go of the need to control at every moment)

These three qualities are all components of the meditation experience. (See Weeks One, Twenty-Six, and Forty respectively.) Not a golfer or a tennis player? Doesn't matter; the lesson is the same. Peak performance in any endeavor often means taking a break from higher levels of cognition, becoming very aware of the experience of the present moment, and letting your inner wisdom guide your decisions.

*

In what areas of your life are you over-thinking things?

In what spaces could you be better served by being *instead of* thinking?

Have you ever had the experience of being in the zone? What did it feel like?

Can you apply that experience to other arenas of your life?

WEEK FORTY-THREE

Awakening and Seeing

The idea of mindfulness is that there is more happening than what we perceive from the thinking mind. There is a deeper level of insight and knowing that comes when we bring our full attention to the present moment. The thirteenth and fourteenth-century Sufi poets wrote bodies of work which capture the experience of awakening more fully through a settled mind.

"In the ocean a lot goes on beneath your eyes," wrote Hafiz.[51] When I am meditating, those words often drift into my consciousness. As I sit for a while, I begin to uncover a whole world of experience that exists just below the surface of my non-mindful life. It's as if I am on a boat looking out over the large sea and all that I'm aware of is the presence of water, light, and shadow. Yet just below me are every imaginable type of fish and plant, along with predator and hunted, life and death…

Steve Jobs described his meditation experience similarly:

> "If you just sit and observe, you will see how restless your mind is. If you try to calm it, it only makes it worse, but over time it does calm, and when it does, there's room to hear more subtle things—that's when your intuition starts to blossom and you start to see things more clearly and be in the present more. Your mind just slows down, and you see a tremendous expanse in the moment. You see so much more than you could see before."[52]

Sitting in stillness enables us to shed the thick layers of distraction and get a deeper look. When we meditate, we open our eyes to the deep, mysterious, and beautiful world otherwise obscured from view.

There are sounds, emotions, tensions in the muscles, and habits of the mind and body, all floating around beneath our consciousness, and then our minds settle and suddenly a whole world, previously hidden, comes to life.

Have you ever been snorkeling and been surprised by what you see underneath the water's surface?

Or have you had a similar experience where a hidden world is revealed through discovery and going deeper into exploration?

What hidden worlds have you uncovered in your meditation practice this week — sounds, sensations, thoughts, feelings?

WEEK FORTY-FOUR

Chanting

Some people like to include chanting as part of their meditation practice. Chanting can be a stand-alone activity which you do in lieu of silent meditation, or it can be a preparation for sitting in silence.

Chanting is typically done through repetition of a mantra (or series of sounds). The mantra or sounds can have a particular meaning, or they might just function as a gateway to creating a particular neural energy. Eastern cultures, where meditation traditions and practices first arose, tend to place a lot of emphasis on the importance of sound and tonality. The word "om," for example (sometimes written "aum"), takes its significance not from any particular meaning, but from the sound it makes, which is said to be the universal sound.

Interestingly, researchers have found that chanting "om" appears to deactivate the limbic part of the brain (by stimulating the vagus nerve: see Week Forty-Eight); thus, chanting appears to create vibrations which help reduce stress, anxiety, and depression.[53] For centuries, chanting has been associated with more blissful mental states.

The trick seems to be to find a chant that has a range of sounds featuring deep humming and originating at the back of the throat. Here are some suggestions:

Traditional Chant: Nam Myoho Renge Kyo

Traditional Chant: Om Mani Padme Hum

Christian Chant: Ma Ra Na Tha[54]

Jewish Chant: Ribono Shel Olam[55]

Here's a mantra created for this week with no meaning or tradition behind it (other than what you choose for yourself): Ha Na Ya Mum.

To practice chanting, set yourself up as you would for meditation—comfortably seated, with your eyes closed. Given that you'll be making sound, you might feel more comfortable sitting somewhere that co-workers or strangers cannot hear you. Set a timer and spend five to ten minutes repeating the mantra of your choice. After you finish, spend a minute or more sitting in stillness and quiet to feel the effects of the chanting on your nervous system, such as a slight tingling sensation in your body or a feeling of calmness.

How does it feel to chant?

What feels good about it?

Did you notice any effects when you sat in silence at the end?

If you went straight to silent meditation after the chanting, did you notice any changes in your meditation practice?

Did you notice any differences in the body?

WEEK FORTY-FIVE

Chakras (Energy Centers) Part One

In the yogic and Ayurvedic traditions there are seven chakras (energy centers) in the body. It is believed that meditating on those seven centers promotes greater emotional, physical, and spiritual health. This week as we meditate, we begin with the first three energy areas (chakras) in our body. Next week we'll focus on the remaining four.

Root Chakra: The first chakra is the root chakra and it exists at the base of spine (tailbone). It's associated with the feeling of safety and security, the color red, the sense perception of smell, and the sound LAM. You can begin your meditation at the base of the spine, turning your attention to the very bottom of the spine where it connects to the floor or the chair while you are seated. For two to three minutes, visualize an aura of red, pay attention to any scents which may be accessible to you, or (silently) chant the sound of LAM. (The *a* in the chanting sounds is flat, more like the sound in lumber than in lamb).

Sacral Chakra: Just below the navel sits the second energy center. The sacral chakra concerns creativity, pleasure, and joy. The color is orange, the sense perception is taste, and the sound is VAM. For two to three minutes, visualize the color orange just below the navel, pay attention to any tastes in your mouth, or chant the sound of VAM. (Again the vowel sound is like a cross between a flat *a* and the *u* in thumb.)

Solar Plexus Chakra: The third chakra is associated with self-confidence, inner drive, and action. It's located in the center of the abdomen (above the navel and below the ribs). If you're feeling like you need to stoke your inner fire, this chakra is where you want to spend more time meditating. The color is a warm yellow, the sense is sight, and the sound is RAM. Take two to four minutes to visualize warm yellow in the center of the abdomen, focus on the sense of sight (even with the eyes closed), or chant the sound RAM.

Did you feel anything different about your body, energy, or attention in this meditation?

Which did you find most effective — the concentration on the physical location in the body, the color visualization, or the sound of the chant?

When you are focusing on an individual chakra, can you feel the association with particular feelings such as safety (root chakra), pleasure and joy (sacral chakra), or self-confidence (solar plexus chakra)?

Chakras (Energy Centers) Part Two

Last week we connected to the first of the three energy centers (Root, Sacral, and Solar Plexis) during our meditation. This week we'll direct our attention to the remaining four.

Heart Chakra: The fourth chakra, located at the center of the chest, heart level, concerns unconditional love, kindness, and compassion. The associated color is green, the sense is touch, and the sound is YAM. (Remember that the sound of the *a* is flat. Yam is said like "yahm" rather than like the orange root vegetable.) Take two to three minutes to focus on the space in the center of the upper chest. As you breathe in, imagine the space filling with the color green, and as you breathe out, make the sound YAM. Or, focus on becoming more aware of the sense of touch and its manifestations as awareness of texture and pressure.

Throat Chakra: If you have trouble with expressing your thoughts and feelings (either you hold back or open up too much), the fifth chakra is a good place to focus. As it suggests, this energy center located in the center of the throat concerns communication and expression of yourself and your ideas. For two to three minutes, as you breathe in, feel the middle of the throat fill with the color blue, and as you breathe out, vocalize the sound HAM (pronounced "hahm"). Or focus on the sense of sound in the present moment. What can you hear from far away, from just outside your room, from within your room, and from within your own body?

Brow Chakra: Often referred to as the Third Eye Chakra, the sixth energy center rests in the area between the brows that overlaps with the pineal gland. The pineal gland is a light preceptor that works somewhat like our two eyes do, picking up awareness of light and dark to help regulate our circadian rhythms (which in turn guide our sleep and wake cycles). In the Ayurvedic system, the brow chakra is associated with wisdom and intuition. As you breathe in, visualize filling the brow center with the color indigo, and as you breathe out chant the sound OM.

Crown Chakra: The seventh and final energy center is the top of the head. The crown chakra marks the space of spiritual connection. By spiritual connection, practitioners of the Ayurvedic system are referring to a person's ability to access the interconnectivity of all of creation. It is a sense of unity and oneness. To deepen your crown chakra, spend two to three minutes breathing in the color violet (into the top of the head), and exhaling the sound OM.

Which chakras feel the most accessible to your awareness?

What did you learn about yourself the last two weeks while practicing the chakra meditations?

What information will be helpful to you in the future? Why?

WEEK FORTY-SEVEN

A Meditation Fable

There's a classic tale of unknown origin about our ability (or inability) to see into the future and know what life has in store for us. Meditation allows us to pause and see the limits of what we know and what we don't.

In a village somewhere there lived a farmer. One day a fence broke and his only horse ran away. The other villagers gathered, shaking their heads, saying, "Bad luck." The farmer replied, "Good luck, bad luck. Who knows?"

A week later his horse returned leading a herd of wild stallions into his field. All the other villagers gathered round and said, "Good luck." The farmer replied, "Good luck, bad luck. Who knows?"

The next week, the farmer's son was breaking in one of the stallions when he fell and broke his leg. The villagers exclaimed, "Very bad luck," and the farmer said, "Good luck, bad luck. Who knows?"

Two days later, the army marched through the village taking any able-bodied boys, and the farmer's son was overlooked due to his injury. The other villagers proclaimed, "Very good luck," to which the farmer replied, "Good luck, bad luck. Who knows?"

In our work and personal lives, how often do we worry about a situation that initially appears to be "bad" or even "horribly terrible," that ends up being anything from "not-so-bad" to "incredibly amazing"? The reason situations can surprise us is that we create stories about what they mean for the long-term. And those stories are just that — stories — because none of us can predict the future with 100% certainty. By staying in the present moment, we can stop ourselves from constructing negative narratives about the future and can, instead, stay open to the constant unfolding of the present, moment by moment.

What do you wish you could know now that you cannot possibly know until a future time?

Have you ever thought that an event or incident was bad luck and it turned out to be good luck, or vice versa?

Where in your life do you tend to presume a particular future outcome that is, upon reflection, not actually knowable?

WEEK FORTY-EIGHT

Breathing and Stress

Some fascinating and still-developing research links a form of breath called *ujjayi* ("ocean breath") to our vagal tone (a measure of how our body responds to stress). Vagal tone refers to the sensitivity of the vagus nerve (the "air traffic controller of the entire nervous system"). People with high vagal tone have nervous systems which recover more quickly from stressful situations. *Ujjayi* breath (which involves the constriction of the back of the throat — the glottis), like humming and chanting, appears to increase vagal tone.

To practice your *ujjayi* breathing (pronounced *you-ji-i*), begin by holding the palm of your hand in front of your mouth as if you were holding a mirror. Next, exhale through your mouth as if you were trying to fog up a mirror. (You can, of course, use a real mirror if you have one available.) Do this two or three times, paying attention to the constricting sensation in the back of your throat. Then close your mouth and do the exhale again. You should hear a sound that some people compare to Darth Vader's breathing or the sound of the ocean in the distance.

The inhale is a little more challenging. The breath should feel as if it's being pulled or vacuumed in from the back of the throat. The tongue may actually become concave as the breath is sucked into the upper back of the throat. The sound of the inhale is more subtle and quiet than the exhale. (If you hear a sniffing sound, you're too far forward in the nostrils.)

Given how loud *ujjayi* breath can sound, I don't recommend practicing it while standing in line for airport security or in other conspicuous and public places.

Another (easier) relaxing and meditative breath exercise is called three-part exhalation. Take a mindful breath in and then exhale one third of the air. Pause. Exhale the second third. Pause. Exhale the final third. Breathe in and repeat.

The next time you are alone in a stressful situation, such as killer traffic or in your office before you're about to make an important presentation, start breathing deeply while constricting the back of the throat and observe how your heart rate begins to slow down. Or try the three-part exhalation technique.

As you practice your ujjayi or three-part exhale breathing, do you notice how just spending a few minutes paying attention to your breath is calming in and of itself?

Are there other times that you tend notice your breath such as after strenuous exercise or in high altitudes? How is this meditative noticing different? Write about your experience with the breath here.

WEEK FORTY-NINE

The Mindfulness Payoff: Invest Ten, Get Thirty or More

Confession time. I haven't done my home practice in five days. (I've been busy and lazy.)

I've noticed that my mind is wandering more and that's slowing down my writing time. It's taking me longer to organize my thoughts and get them on paper. Instead of taking about two hours to write my monthly column for work, it's taken me almost four. And this morning, as I was driving to a corporate client, I got lost in thoughts about an event this afternoon and I ended getting off the highway at the wrong exit. That little mistake cost me fifteen minutes and a lot of stress.

In contrast, when I'm engaged in regular meditation practice, I spend less time looking for misplaced keys, reading glasses, or phone. I also spend less time going upstairs to do something and then forgetting what it was that I needed to do.

Though sometimes ten minutes a day seems like too much time, it's an investment that in both the short and long run saves me so much more. If you could invest $10 a day with a guaranteed return of $30 a day, would you do it? Of course you would.

Mindfulness works the same way. Invest ten to fifteen minutes a day and get so much more time back in return. There are only 24 hours in a day and only about sixteen of those are waking hours, but we can get the most out of each of those sixteen hours by having a clear and focused mind.

On days when you don't meditate, do you notice a difference in your ability to pay attention?

Overall, do you notice a before and after difference in your ability to pay attention since you've begun a regular practice?

WEEK FIFTY

The Universal Experiences of Mindfulness

At one of my corporate clients where I send out a weekly mindfulness blog, people frequently stop me in the hallway and ask, "Was your blog the other week directed at me?" Typically, I pause and try figure out which blog they're referring to, even though my answer 9.9 out of ten times is no.

The great thing about this reaction to my blog, and to mindfulness in general, is that people feel it IS speaking to them. The reason it's speaking to them (to all of us) is because our needs, fears, hopes, and frustrations are usually not unique to us; they are part of the larger human experience.

Typically, when people first encounter meditation they talk about how hard it is for THEM, because THEIR mind is crazy busy—as if no one else has an active mind. The truth is that all of our minds are busy; it's a biological fact that human brains are programmed to be active. Neurologists even refer to the chattering mind as the "default-mode network." In fact, the human brain's ability to ruminate about the past and plan the future has helped the human species to survive and thrive. The capacity to apply the complex lessons learned from past experiences to future plans is at the heart of our impressive cognitive tool-kit.

But like all good things, there's a price for all of that thinking. Humans are also prone to high levels of depression and anxiety (which are directly related to worry and regret types of thinking). This helps explain why some of the most successful forms of non-pharmacological therapy for treating depression and anxiety (Cognitive Behavioral Therapy and its derivatives) employ mindfulness practices as a means of reducing excessive past and future thinking.

Because the evolution of the human brain as a busy hub for so much thinking affects us all, our experience with mindfulness is very universal. In other words, meditation challenges *all* of us to be present in our lives as much as possible.

How much do worry and regret occupy your thinking?

As you meditate this week, pay attention to your thoughts as they come up. Are they about the past (rumination) or the future (planning)?

WEEK FIFTY-ONE

When Less is More

Typically, I wake up in the morning and before I've even brushed my teeth or had a chance to think about what I'm going to wear, I get right to my meditation practice. A few months ago I found myself actually dreading my daily sit, which led me to wonder what had happened to so dramatically changed my feelings about meditation.

A mentor's post on social media (who says social media is all bad?) on letting go during meditation solved the mystery. I realized I had started struggling in my practice to quiet my mind. And the more effort and struggle I generated, the less benefit I received. Meditation is about letting go of effort and just being with what is. Instead, I had let my Type A tendencies take over my meditation practice. It's not unusual for most of us, at some time, to let the search for a solution become part of the problem, creating an absurdity: we create stress through our efforts to de-stress.

Many successful, high-achieving people like you suffer from over-efforting. You work hard, exercise hard, housework hard, parent hard, leisure hard... and I imagine that you might also approach meditation with the same intensity.

Instead, approach your meditation practice this week with an eye toward letting go of all effort and any desire for a particular outcome, eventually letting go of even the letting go. Just show up and see what happens, moment by moment.

Can you notice the connection between non-efforting in your practice and feeling less stress in other parts of your life?

Where in your life might you be over-efforting? Write down your observations here.

Awareness of Our Story-Telling

Humans are sense-making animals. Our minds are always working to interpret and make sense of our world. For example, on Saturday night I was at a concert and was seated right in front of the stage. Though I was really enjoying the music, with such an up-close view I was also intrigued by the subtle communication going on among the band members themselves and also with the audience and the sound crew. What did that facial expression by the bass player mean? Is the lead singer frustrated with the sound crew guy or just ignoring him? On and on, the sense-making work went. Of course, whatever answers I came up with were just stories I was telling myself. I could decide that the bass player was confused, playful, or had indigestion.

Recognizing how much of our world is story-making is liberating. On Sunday nights we can tell ourselves a story about our work week that can either make us excited for Monday morning or cause us to feel dread. Observing how the mind works is part of what mindfulness is all about.

When we are sitting in the present moment and noticing what we are experiencing, we can also become aware of the stories we are creating moment by moment. You might hear the wail of a siren and begin to formulate a story about the neighborhood you live or work in, or about where the siren is heading or what the emergency is about. You might even begin to notice that the story begins when you place words and labels around the present moment experience. Instead of hearing a siren, just hear the sound itself, the pitch, the pattern, the experience of the sound getting closer and then farther away. Pay attention to the present moment experiences as they stand without adding layers of added narrative.

So much of what we practice in meditation, if not all of it, provides important tools for living our daily lives. Noticing the stories which emerge while we meditate allows us to observe the story-making that is constantly unfolding in our day-to-day experience. Detaching from and observing narratives when they arise empowers us to create what we want or need. In other words, our meditation offers us liberation; we get to choose the stories we create in our minds, and we can choose stories which inspire and bring greater joy and peace into our lives and the lives of others.

In the past, what stories have you told yourself about yourself, stories that have not served you well?

What about stories about other people or events which affected you?

How differently would your life be transpiring if you were more aware of how often you generate stories in your head?

Section 6

Meditations for Special Moments During the Year

THE NEW YEAR

Begin Again

The countdown to midnight on New Year's Eve creates the sense that something profound is taking place. We're wrapping up another year of our life, with pride, regret, or nostalgia. And then we turn with great hope to the new year about to unfold.

Mindfulness meditation has a lot to teach about how we handle endings and beginnings and the transition between the two. While you're sitting quietly, observing your breath, pay particular attention to the transitions between your inhale and your exhale. What happens when you move from breathing in to breathing out and back again? What does it feel like in your lungs and diaphragm? Where does the movement begin: in your chest, nose or belly?

The practice of sitting also teaches us that at any moment we can begin again. We start our meditation with our mind on our breath and then, predictably, our mind wanders. As soon as we notice the mind wandering, we bring it back to the present to begin again. We learn that we can begin again at any time we choose. The reset button is always there.

If you haven't done so already, take some time this week to mindfully reflect on your accomplishments from last year and make a list of them all (big and small). Then take some time to reflect on your hopes for the new year. How do you want to grow as a person? How do you want to grow in your relationships with other important people in your life? With your friends? With strangers? How can you live healthier and more in harmony with the planet?

How can meditation and mindfulness be a part of the resolutions you set for your life in the upcoming year?

How can you recommit or stay committed to your meditation practice in the new year?

How does your practice help you see that actions build on each other (such as how meditation helps you improve other parts of your life)?

LATE JANUARY

A Late January Perspective
on New Years' Resolutions

January 1st of every year feels so full of possibility. Through the simple counting down of the clock to midnight and a change in the number at the end of the date, we commit to big and small changes: losing weight, repairing relationships, advancing in our careers, or acquiring a new hobby. The new year feels not quite a blank slate, but about as close as to one as a human being can get.

By the end of January, though, we start to become discouraged about the good intentions that weren't so easy for us to fulfill. Perhaps you had committed to losing weight, eating healthier, being more organized, getting more exercise, or even initiating a personal meditation practice. Yet after a couple of enthusiastic weeks, you've found yourself off-track.

Our meditation practice teaches us that each and every moment is an opportunity to hit the reset button. You can begin again at any time. Our mind wanders and we bring it back and then it wanders and we bring it back. And each time we bring it back we are starting again—with patience and non-judgment.

There is nothing magical about January 1st. What is a year but the full orbit of the earth around the sun? Not quite a circle but an ellipse, without beginning or end, or, rather, infinite points of beginnings and endings. In other words, any day (at any point in the orbit) we can begin again. In fact, every moment in time from when you rise in the morning until you go to bed at night can be a time to begin again. January 31st at 7:00 AM works just as well (if not better) as a good time to begin again. And in fact, this very moment as you are reading this very word is a great moment to begin again, as is this moment, and this moment…

Use this week to practice the art of beginning again.

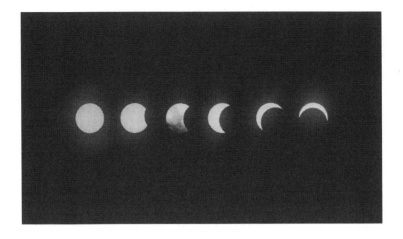

What resolution did you make earlier in the month that you would like to begin again?

What resolution(s) do you want to begin with this week?

With what else in your life could you employ the attitude of "begin again" for greater happiness and success?

VALENTINE'S DAY

Why *Metta* Meditation Is So Good for You

We often think of Valentine's Day as a celebration of romantic love. Partners surprise each other with flowers, chocolate, or dinner out on the town. But as meditators, we know that love is more than just a feeling we have for special people in our lives. Cultivating love and compassion for all people — in fact, all beings — is a common focus of meditation. Week Seven introduced *metta* meditation. *Metta* means "loving-kindness" in Pali (a sacred language).

What is interesting about *metta* meditation is its effect on the practitioner. Love is often thought to make us happier, and that is true, but practicing just seven minutes of *metta* meditation has been found to make people kinder and more caring.[56] Loving-kindness meditation doesn't just make you feel differently about others' suffering, it also makes you more likely to act on those feelings, offering help to those in need.[57]

This Valentine's Day, take your cue from your *metta* meditation and extend your sense of love and compassion beyond your inner circle. Find ways of expressing a loving heart for people you barely know, people who vex you, people you've never met, and for all living creatures.

How can you express love and caring to people in your life in a way that feels deep and genuine?

What are some good ways to express love and compassion to people outside of your inner circle?

What ways can you bring love and compassion into your own life throughout the year?

SUMMER

Mindfulness Outdoors

Weekends, vacations, and summertime are great times to recommit to quieting your mind, especially from the worries of the world of work and career. To make the most of the great weather that summer brings, spend more of your meditation time outside. There are all kinds of studies that conclude that time in nature is good for our health. Venturing out into nature is associated with improved memory, mood, concentration, mental energy, eyesight, creativity, and immune system functioning, and lower levels of stress and inflammation.[58] Here are two opportunities to combine the benefits of being in the outdoors with those of meditation practice.

Slow Mindful Walk: Find a safe path to walk, away from other people, where you can be alone without concern. Then walk as slowly as you can. (Mindful walking is not about raising your heart rate or burning calories.) Notice how when you're walking you shift your balance from right foot to left foot and back again. When you're walking slowly, balance actually becomes slightly more challenging. Notice how your weight shifts from heel to toe. You might also want to use your slow pace to become aware of whether you tend to pronate (stand mainly on the inside edges of your feet) or supinate (bear most of your weight standing on the outside edges of your feet).

While you are walking, take time to observe the details of your surroundings, using all of your senses. Look down at the ground and up to the sky. Listen to sounds from close by and far away. Feel the sensation of air on your skin or in your lungs. Stay aware of the smells you encounter on your walk.

Campfire: An ancient form of meditation involves focusing on the mesmerizing flicker of flames. An outdoor campfire is a great opportunity to practice a focused awareness meditation (although a fire in the fireplace, or even a candle, works just as well). Watch the fire in silence and stillness, noticing the various colors of light and the sounds of the fire consuming the wood. This isn't a campfire for s'mores or singing, although that can come after you spend time just being in the experience.

What do you enjoy most about being outdoors?

What emotions do you tend to experience while walking alone in nature or watching a campfire in the dark and silence?

How is meditating on the movement and color of a fire different than meditating with your eyes closed?

INDEPENDENCE DAY

Freedom and Risk

On July 2, 1776, the Second Continental Congress voted to declare independence from England and signed the formal document two days later. The signers knew they were risking their lives when they signed the document, but they did so boldly and bravely.

Change (freeing ourselves from the patterns of the past) generally requires a degree of risk and uncertainty. We don't know if our efforts will be successful or if the changes will bring us the outcome we want—a better situation than the previous one.

Consider meditation and mindfulness as breaks from the way we typically engage with the present moment. Normally, we only check in with the present when it storms our consciousness with intense experiences (such as riding a roller coaster or watching the birth of our children) or when compelled to (say, while listening to a lecture which we will be tested on afterwards). Mindfulness invites us to have a different, more intentional relationship with the present at any given moment.

The freedom from our regular patterns of thinking feels risky, but ultimately, we have more to gain by declaring our independence from our stream-of-conscious thoughts. We will live more fully, and with greater awareness of those subconscious habits of the mind that can undermine our career success, sabotage our relationships, and drown us in our emotions. When we work to become more mindful, we are also exercising the freedom to live with more conscious choice and action. All we need is to be bold and brave like our national forefathers.

Happy Independence Day!

What are you willing to risk in order to have change in your life?

What do you make of the quote, "Hint: The cage is not locked," by Nova Knutson?

What are the stories you tell yourself about change?

HALLOWEEN

Removing the Masks

Halloween is time when many people don masks to cover their faces. The rest of the year, though, many of us are wearing masks that we aren't even aware of until we become very quiet and still. When we begin to have a regular meditation practice, we start to notice how the muscles in our face relax and soften as we sit in silence with our eyes closed. It begins to feel as if the mask we've been wearing around in the world is melting away and our true self is emerging.

There's a lovely Swedish folk tale about a princess who is, against her will, about to be wed to a dragon. Just before the wedding day, the princess, terrified for her life, seeks the counsel of a wise old woman. The wise woman assures the princess that she will be safe but that she must wear nine layers of gowns underneath her wedding gown.

The next night, after the ceremony, the dragon and the princess retire to his room to consummate their nuptials. The princess consents but first, she says, the dragon must agree to remove a layer of his garments for every layer she removes. The dragon agrees. The princess removes her wedding gown and the dragon peels away the outer layer of his skin, which from time to time molts off anyway. Then the princess removes her next gown. The dragon does the same. By the fifth layer, the dragon is weeping in pain, but still the princess, following the guidance of the wise old woman, continues to remove layers of gown, followed by the dragon. Each layer the dragon removes, the skin beneath is softer, less prickly. The dragon removes his final layer and reveals himself to be a prince, now fully human.

For many of us, meditation works the same. We remove layers of our rigid, hardened self to reveal the soft and royal true person trapped inside.

Who is the real you trapped inside a dragon?

In what ways are you like the princess, helping others to change by modeling change in yourself?

The dragon needed to shed his skin to reveal his true self. What do you need to let go of to find your true self?

Reflect on the idea that change can be painful.

THANKSGIVING

Gratitude

In the chaos of holiday preparation, sometimes we focus exclusively on the travel and food to the extent that we forget the *thanks* in Thanksgiving. That's a shame, because neurologists and psychologists know that the feeling of gratitude is an emotional power house. It heightens our emotional well-being in numerous ways.

To understand how gratitude rewires your brain consider the word itself. The Latin root of "gratitude" is *gratus*, which means thankful or pleasing. When we make a practice out of looking for the good, we begin to train our mind to see goodness in the world. Researchers in one study found that, after ten weeks of gratitude practice, participants had fewer doctor visits, scored higher on tests of optimism, and were more likely to exercise and get better sleep. Other studies on the effects of gratitude have found a positive association with increased happiness.[59]

This week, bring a sense of gratitude to your meditation practice by noting what you feel grateful for in the present moment while you're sitting.

Here are a few other ways you can bring more gratitude into your life:

Keep a Gratitude Journal. Every night or morning, spend a few minutes writing a list of three to five things for which you feel grateful.

Make it a weekly practice to write two or three thank you notes. While the effort of handwriting a note has a positive impact for both the sender and the recipient, don't discount email as an alternative.

Say thanks for the many little blessings throughout the day—waking up, before meals, after meals, when you arrive back home, when you turn on lights, when you get a call, email or text from someone you care about. No blessing is too small to ignore.

What can you be grateful for in this present moment?

What practice of gratitude will you commit to this week, in addition to your mindfulness practice?

What did you learn about yourself in your practice this week?

DECEMBER

Mindful Eating for the Holidays

Early December (aka "holiday season") is a good time to practice a form of meditation called mindful eating. Like all forms of mindfulness, an eating meditation requires us to be fully aware of what is happening in the present moment. There's a special level of deliberateness to this practice, as you will see. Here are the steps to mindful eating:

Be aware of the motivating factor behind your decision to eat. Are you hungry, or are you just bored or feeling socially awkward?

Look at your food before you eat it. Notice its texture, color, size, and shape.

Smell your food. What aroma, if any, does it give off before you put it in your mouth?

Chew your food very slowly, noticing all of the taste sensations (sweet, salty, sour, and bitter), textures (crunchy, smooth, etc.), and sounds (loud or silent).

Pause between bites and reflect on the pleasantness of the food you have eaten. Also, take a moment to notice if you are feeling sated or still hungry. If you decide to keep eating, go back to step one and repeat the process.

By eating mindfully, you eat more slowly and deliberately. You have more time to notice when you're feeling full so you'll be less likely to eat more than you should. Also, eating mindfully makes you more aware of the pleasure you get out of the eating experience — the tastes and textures of your food — giving you a greater sense of satisfaction with each morsel of food you eat. And enjoying the food is really what the chefs and hosts want you to do.

Can you practice eating your next meal or snack using all five steps?

What is the experience like for you?

What emotions does mindful eating elicit?

How can you bring mindful eating to your experience of eating throughout the year?

How do mindful eating and gratitude work together?

END OF THE YEAR

Preparing for the New Year

If you've been slacking off in the regularity of your meditation practice or have dropped it altogether, the time between Thanksgiving and New Year's Day is a good time to rev up your commitment. The end of the calendar year presents us with two challenges: holiday season and preparing for the year ahead. The practice of meditation offers two perfect solutions to these specific challenges: stillness and insight.

Stillness: The holiday season is tough (even if you don't celebrate Christmas, Chanukah, or Kwanzaa). The days are getting noticeably shorter and darker, and at the same time, we're all dealing with crowded malls, supermarkets and parking lots, gift-giving lists which can feel overwhelming, traveling, time with extended family, parties and entertaining... We need a little antidote to the frantic busyness that mindfulness meditation offers. It's the perfect respite of stillness and quiet. When we get busy, often the first things to go are the self-care routines which we need more than usual. Give yourself the holiday gift of daily meditation practice this week.

Insight: As we count down the days to the end of this current year, we begin to reflect on the year (its successes and its challenges) and start to sketch out how we'd like the next year to transpire (our hopes and desires). Mindfulness meditation helps us reflect and refine our values, and teaches us to observe without judgment. It creates the space for us to sit and listen to our inner self declare its truest intentions. With this insight, we can learn from the year that is ending and lay the groundwork for our greatest success in the coming year.

How will calmness and stillness help you navigate the holiday season this year?

What insights are you looking for as you think about your year?

Can you write down five accomplishments you made in the past year?

What do you hope to accomplish in the year to come?

CONCLUSION

The most important conclusion I want you to come to at the end of a year of meditating is that you want to keep going, making meditation a part of your daily routine for the rest of your life. In other words, there is no conclusion, just a beginning again. As with our meditation practice itself, the bell rings, we begin, we drift, we begin again, we drift, we begin again, the bell rings, we drift, the bell rings, we begin, we drift, we begin again... It's a cyclical and on-going effort to forge a strong relationship between our conscious self and the present moment.

If reaching this point in the book is not truly a conclusion, then let it be a moment to pause and reflect on the experience of the year. Every endeavor, especially a new one, has its highlights and challenges. Let's start by acknowledging the challenges you faced maintaining a regular practice (however you define regular). Thinking back on the year, what were the top three challenges?

1. _____

2. _____

3. _____

It's important to remember that we all confront obstacles to doing what we need to do, even if the actions make us feel better. When we need to get up early and head to the gym, the snooze button can be awfully easy to hit numerous times. When we need to pass on dessert, the sweet tooth in us starts screaming louder. We confront the desire to stay in the status quo because it's easier and familiar, but we can show up in a powerful way when we find the courage and discipline to change.

Despite the challenges to establishing and maintaining a consistent mindful mediation practice, to what degree were you able to address them? How were you able to overcome those challenges? Or, if you weren't, how might you address them in the year to come?

_____

_____

_____

_____

_____

Underlying my hope that you continue your meditation practice is the trust that you've realized that the effort and commitment are worth it because the net positive results are tremendous. Meditation offers a range of benefits for practitioners. Some benefits are measurable, such as lower blood pressure, but most benefits are going to be subtle or subjectively experienced by each individual. I hope you have concluded that a consistent practice has improved your life. Thinking back over the year, did you notice any changes in your relationships with others (such as your kids, spouse, partner, colleagues, superiors, direct reports)? How about in your general happiness and your sense of calm and contentment? Have you felt less stress this year? What were the top five beneficial outcomes of your regular meditation practice that you noticed this year? Give examples, if possible.

1. _____

_____

2. _____

_____

3. _____

_____

4. _____

_____

5. _____

_____

Reflecting back on the year, how would you summarize your experience with meditation?

_____

_____

_____

What victories did you accomplish in your practice?

_____

_____

_____

What time of day did you find the best for fitting meditation into your schedule?

_____

What physical space did you find the most conducive to your practice? Do you like to be somewhere completely quiet or a place with low level or intermittent sound?

_____

What strategies for quieting the mind did you find most effective?

_____

_____

_____

What type of meditation did you practice most or find the most fruitful?

_____

_____

_____

In thinking about the year ahead, what are your hopes and expectations for your life in general, and how can your meditation practice help you meet your goals?

_____

_____

_____

_____

As you contemplate the year ahead, what plans do you have for your meditation practice?

_____

_____

Finally, how can you maintain your commitment? What can you do to improve the consistency of your practice? Have you considered attending a meditation retreat or attending a workshop? Are there other books you might consider reading to help you further your practice and feel more fully engaged? Chart out your next year of mindfulness practice here:

_____

_____

_____

_____

_____

What is the next step in your meditation practice, after you turn over the last page of this book? Perhaps it's to turn the book over again to start back on page one. Or it may be that you set sail on another sea of experience and guidance. Either way, remember that your practice is always available to you at any moment. Forgot to mediate this morning or this month? No problem. Just find a quiet place for a few moments to close your eyes and quiet your mind. The practice isn't easy; the rewards are immeasurable.

APPENDIX A

How to Create a Calm Room for the Workplace (or Home)

Every job comes with stressors, and sometimes we even show up to work feeling stressed from our commute, from getting our kids off to school, from getting ourselves out the door, from challenges in our personal life, both big and small. Add in the pressures of the job itself, with deadlines, office politics, and maddening updates to the technology, and sometimes we need a moment to collect ourselves to get centered and grounded.

When your emotional barometric pressure rises and you feel as if you're either going to explode or implode, where can you go to internally reorganize? If you ever spent time in the restroom at work simply because it was the only place available for you to be alone with your thoughts without the phone ringing or someone knocking on your door, or if you or your employees do not have private offices, then you might consider setting up a calm room in your workplace. A calm room can be created using space that is already available, such as a lactation room. Some workplaces combine the space assigned for new mothers to pump with a place for employees to de-stress. Or, a room can be converted from its present usage — say a phone booth, a storage room, or an empty office. Some companies build a calm room into their remodeling blue prints. However you secure the space to create a calm room, the same design characteristics apply. You want a room that provides privacy, quiet, peacefulness, and comfort.

Privacy

Ideally, pick a location that is off the beaten path, away from office traffic. People should feel like they can enter and exit without calling attention to themselves. The room should also afford privacy with a door that closes shut (but doesn't lock) and without windows that allow others to see inside the room. A great office policy is to

keep the door open when not in use and closed when in use, offer a sign-up sheet to reserve the space, and/or place a "do not disturb" sign on the doorknob when in use.

Quiet

The best location for a calm room is a place where noises from inside or outside of the office are minimal. Again, putting the room off the beaten path will help with noise reduction. There are room modifications that can be made to mitigate noise. Peaceful music can be piped in or made available by providing a speaker system, which can be switched on or off, that plays a select type of music. The challenge with music can be choosing something that appeals to a wide range of folks. Consider music that might be played while someone is getting a massage. In fact, there is a whole genre of relaxing music to tap into, along with music subscription services. Noise cancelling or white noise machines are another possibility, and desktop or wall fountains can also be added to the space. In the end, though, consider that pure silence might be what people are most seeking and need.

Peaceful

Sometimes the words we ascribe to our lives include frantic, over-scheduled, harried, busy, sensory-overloaded, and demanding. The calm room should be the antithesis of all of that. Keep the decor warm, yet minimal. The calm room should have low and natural lighting. It should feel clean and tidy, but not antiseptic like a hospital waiting room. The decor should contain soothing color tones. The specifics of which colors to choose will depend on the fashion of the day, but generally more muted hues are more peaceful. Stick to one wall color and even accent colors should be subdued.

Living plants are also a nice touch. As humans, we respond to being around plants that absorb carbon dioxide and send out oxygen during the day. Being in a room with a plant or two can make us feel reinvigorated and brings nature back into an otherwise completely human-fabricated domain. There is some research which suggests that indoor plants have a positive impact on people's mental health.[60]

Comfortable

Sitting in the room should embody the feeling of self-care because the act of taking a break from your work to tend to your inner self is, indeed, an act of caregiving to yourself. A calm room should communicate a feeling of conscious relaxation and warmth.

People sitting in the room should feel comfortable, but not too comfortable. We don't recommend chaise lounges or any seating arrangement that takes people into a reclining or fully supine position. Most people do not want to be seen as literally "sleeping on the job."

Ideally, room temperature should be adjustable, but if it isn't, make sure the calm room is not in a location that is prone to temperature extremes. Adding scents to the room is risky for the same reason that wearing cologne at work is discouraged. People can be turned off, offended, or allergic to certain fragrances. That being said, scents are very emotionally evocative and can help put people in a state of feeling calm and relaxed. In practice, I've found that most people appreciate a light scent of lavender or sandalwood, but you'll need to tread lightly and get a feel for the needs of your particular office culture.

ACKNOWLEDGMENTS

Writing a book is never fully a story of a solitary person locked in a room feverishly tapping away on a keyboard. Someone needs to remind the writer to eat lunch or go for a walk, and someone needs to comfort or coach the writer through many moments of doubt and confusion. Writing done the correct way also involves various sets of eyes and multiple rounds of feedback. A fortunate writer, in fact has a team of support from start to finish.

I've been very lucky with this book. I've had the blessing from the start from everyone at Rewire: Steve Scanlon, Jason Abell, Steve Longan, Stef Sample, Rafa Scanlon, Paolo Scanlon, Stuart Tyrie, Jay Morton, Kate Gigax and all of the new coaches. Stephanie Wetherby deserves a big applause. She has unquestionably delivered as the brilliant and creative editor. It was her direction which shaped the content from a random collection of blog writings into a cohesive final product. Praise and thanks also go to my teachers: Steve Haddad, Rabbi Jeff Roth, and Sheila H. Katz. Any errors in this book are strictly my own.

Other people who have contributed to the making of *The Art of Being Present* are the crew of clients for whom these weekly writings were originally intended. I want to specifically thank Lesley McQuillan, John B. Frisch, Tim McDermond, Emma Neuse, Dana Gloor, Catherine Mudd, Kris Holland, Josh Brickman, Karene Hansen, Bob Woodson, Kymbrely Piper, Tom LaFleur, Ashley DeSantis, Andrew Patterson, Ryan Doyle, Maryam Seveur, Megan Burnett, Karen Cringoli, Diane Leiner, Joanne Jones, Adolphus Gwynn, Andrea Kehoe, Stacia Krupa, and Aja McNeil. There are many others connected to these groups whom I failed to mention but who were also instrumental. Thank you all for being very open with me about your experiences with work, life, and the practice of mindfulness.

A special nod to Dina Billian who was an early believer in workplace meditation and in my ability to offer it. Another such nod to Tom Kelly for his willingness to dive right in with a meditation practice and become a believer himself. I'm also grateful for the friendship and opinions of Maggins Kenney, Taylor Owen, Jill Max, Melissa Cordish, Jane Marion, and Loren Duffey.

Finally, always... Parker and Naomi who are the reason I practice mindfulness for all of the benefits. Children make you want to be a better person, and every time I sit, I do it to be a better mother and human. Thank you both for inspiring me just through your very existence.

ENDNOTES

Introduction

1. Jon Kabat-Zinn, *Mindfulness for Beginners: Reclaiming the Present Moment and Your Life* (Boulder: Sounds True, 2006), 1.

2. Joshua Gowin, "Brain Scans Show How Meditation Improves Mental Focus," *Psychology Today*, April 2, 2012, accessed July 7, 2018, https://www.psychologytoday.com/blog/you-illuminated/201204/brain-scans-show-how-meditation-improves-mental-focus.

3. James Hamblin, "Study: Meditation Improves Memory, Attention," *Atlantic Monthly*, May 6, 2013, accessed May 3, 2018, http://www.theatlantic.com/health/archive/2013/05/study-meditation-improves-memory-attention/275564.

4. B. K. Holzel et al., "Mindfulness Practice Leads to Increases in Regional Brain Gray Matter Density," *Psychiatry Research* 191, no. 1 (January 2011): 36-43, accessed April 8, 2018, https://dx.doi.org/10.1016/j.pscychresns.2010.08.006.

5. Tom Jacobs, "Mindfulness Training Produces Less-Stressed Marines," *Pacific Standard*, May 15, 2014, accessed June 3, 2018, http://www.psmag.com/books-and-culture/mindfulness-training-produces-less-stressed-marines-81633.

6. Daphne M. Davis and Jeffrey Hays, "What Are the Benefits of Mindfulness," *American Psychological Association* 43, no. 7 (August 2012): 64.

7. Natalia Karelaia, "How Mindfulness Improves Decision-Making," *Forbes*, August 5, 2014, accessed June 15, 2018, http://www.forbes.com/sites/insead/2014/08/05/how-mindfulness-improves-decision-making.

8. Eileen Luders et al., "The Unique Brain Anatomy of Meditation Practitioners: Alterations in Cortical Gyrification," *Frontiers in Human Neuroscience* 6, no. 34 (February 2012): accessed on June 15, 2018, https://doi.org/10.3389/fnhum.2012.00034.

9. David Gelles, *Mindful Work* (New York: Houghton Mifflin Harcourt, 2015), 77. See also p. 94.

10. Stacy Lu, "Mindfulness Holds Promise for Treating Depression: New Research Suggests Practicing Mindfulness May Help Prevent a Relapse," *APA Monitor on Psychology* 46, no. 3 (March 2015): 50, accessed May

13, 2018, http://www.apa.org/monitor/2015/03/cover-mindfulness.aspx.

11.   Fadel Zeidan et al., "Neural Correlates of Mindfulness Meditation-Related Anxiety Relief," *Social Cognitive and Affective Neuroscience* 9, no. 6 (June 2014): 751–759, accessed May 13, 2018, https://doi.org/10.1093/scan/nst041.

12.   American Heart Association, "Meditation and Heart Health," accessed May 14, 2018, http://www.heart.org/HEARTORG/Conditions/More/MyHeartandStrokeNews/Meditation-and-Heart-Disease-Stroke_UCM_452930_Article.jsp#.VkDSqoTnv44.

13.   Jon Kabat-Zinn et al., "Influence of a Mindfulness Meditation-Based Stress Reduction Intervention on Rates of Skin Clearing in Patients with Moderate to Severe Psoriasis Undergoing Photo Therapy (UVB) and Photochemotherapy (PUVA)," *Psychosomatic Medicine* 60, no. 5 (Sept-Oct 1998): 625-632, accessed June, 2018, https://doi.org/10.3389/fimmu.2017.00670.

14.   Ivana Buric et al., "What Is the Molecular Signature of Mind–Body Interventions? A Systematic Review of Gene Expression Changes Induced by Meditation and Related Practices," *Frontiers in Immunology* 8 (June 2017): 670, accessed March 5, 2018, https://doi.org/10.3389/fimmu.2017.00670.

15.   Marianne T. Marcus and Aleksandra Zgierska, "Mindfulness-Based Therapies for Substance Use Disorders: Part 1 (Editorial)," *Substance Abuse* 30, no. 4 (December 2009): 263, accessed July 1, 2018, https://dx.doi.org/10.1080%2F08897070903250027.

Week One: The Beginning

16.   Kabat-Zinn, *Mindfulness for Beginners*, 1.

Week Six: The Science Supporting Mindfulness ad Meditation

17.   Ivana Buric et al., "Molecular Signature of Mind–Body Interventions," 670.

18.   Daniel Goleman and Richard Davidson, *Altered Traits* (New York: Avery, 2017), 138-139.

19.   Elizabeth Hogue et al., "Randomized Controlled Trial of Mindfulness Meditation for Generalized Anxiety Disorder," *Journal of Clinical Psychiatry* 74, no. 8 (August 2013): 786–792, accessed May 12, 2018, https://doi.org/10.4088/JCP.12m08083.

20. W. Kuyken, "Efficacy of Mindfulness-Based Cognitive Therapy in Prevention of Depressive Relapse: An Individual Patient Data Meta-analysis from Randomized Trials," *JAMA Psychiatry* 73, no. 6, (June 2016): 565-574, accessed May 31, 2018, https://doi.org/10.1001/jamapsychiatry.2016.0076.

21. Símon Guendelman, Sebastian Madeiros, and Hagen Rampes, "Mindfulness and Emotion Regulation: Insights from Neurobiological, Psychological, and Clinical Studies," *Frontiers in Psychology* 8 (March 2017): 220, accessed April 17, 20118, https://doi.org/10.3389/fpsyg.2017.00220.

22. A.B. Fennell, E.M. Benau, and R.A. Atchley, "A Single Session of Meditation Reduces Physiological Indices of Anger in Both Experienced and Novice Meditators," *Consciousness and Cognition* 40 (February 2016): 54-66, accessed May 12, 2018, https://doi.org/10.1016/j.concog.2015.12.010.

23. Mark Wheeler, "Forever Young: Meditation Might Slow Age-Related Loss of Gray Matter in the Brain, Say UCLA Researchers" *UCLA Newsroom*, February 5, 2015, accessed July 2, 2018, http://newsroom.ucla.edu/releases/forever-young-meditation-might-slow-the-age-related-loss-of-gray-matter-in-the-brain-say-ucla-researchers.

24. C. Dunn et al., "Mindfulness Approaches and Weight Loss, Weight Maintenance, and Weight Regain," *Current Obesity Reports* 1 (March 2018): 37-49, accessed June 4, 2018, https://doi.org/10.1007/s13679-018-0299-6.

25. Becka Kelley, "Overcoming Emotional Eating," *Center for Nutrition Studies*, January 14, 2014, accessed July 8, 2018, https://nutritionstudies.org/overcoming-emotional-eating.

26. Y.Y. Tang, R. Tang, and M.I. Posner, "Mindfulness Meditation Improves Emotion Regulation and Reduces Drug Abuse," *Drug and Alcohol Dependence* 163, Supplement 1 (June 1, 2016): S13-S18, accessed July 8, 2018, https://doi.org/10.1016/j.drugalcdep.2015.11.041.

27. Sarah Bowen et al., "Relative Efficacy of Mindfulness-Based Relapse Prevention, Standard Relapse Prevention, and Treatment as Usual for Substance Use Disorders," *JAMA Psychiatry* 71, no. 5 (May 2014): 547-556, accessed May 16, 2018, https://doi.org/10.1001/jamapsychiatry.2013.4546.

Week 18: Real Questions About Meditation

28. Norman A. Farb, Adam K. Anderson, and Zindel V. Segal, "The

Mindful Brain and Emotional Regulation in Mood Disorders," *Canadian Journal of Psychiatry* 57, no. 2 (February 2012): 70-107, accessed July 8, 2018, https://dx.doi.org/10.1177%2F070674371205700203.

Week Nineteen: Do It For the Team

29.   A. Ariga and A. Lleras, "Brief and Rare Mental 'Breaks' Keep You Focused: Deactivation and Reactivation of Task Goals Preempt Vigilance Decrements," *Journal of Cognition* 118, no.3 (March 2011): 439-443, accessed July 8, 2018, https://doi.org/10.1016/j.cognition.2010.12.007.

30.   M. Mrazek et al., "Mindfulness Training Improves Working Memory Capacity and GRE Performance While Reducing Mind Wandering," *Psychological Science* 24, no.5 (May 2013): 1-6, accessed July 8, 2018, https://doi.org/10.1177/0956797612459659.

31.   R. Teper and M. Inzlicht, "Meditation, Mindfulness and Executive Control: The Importance of Emotional Acceptance and Brain-Based Performance Monitoring," *Social Cognitive and Affective Neuroscience* 8, no. 1(January 2013): 85–92, accessed July 8, 2018, https://doi.org/10.1093/scan/nss045.

Week Twenty: Better Decision-Making

32.   Andrew C. Hafenbrack, Zoe Kinias, and Sigal G. Barsade, "Debiasing the Mind Through Meditation: Mindfulness and the Sunk-Cost Bias," *Psychological Science* 25, No. 2 (February 2014): 369-376, accessed September 22, 2018, https://doi.org/10.1177/0956797613503853.

33.   U. Kirk, J. Downar, and P.R. Montague, "Interoception Drives Increased Rational Decision-Making in Meditators Playing the Ultimatum Game," *Frontiers in Neuroscience* 18, no.5 (April 2011): 49, accessed July 8, 2018, https://doi.org/10.3389/fnins.2011.00049.

Week Twenty-One: Happiness and Productivity

34.   Daniel Sgroi, "Happiness and productivity: Understanding the Happy-Productive Worker," (University of Warwick Centre for Competitive Advantage in the Global Economy, Global Perspectives Series, October 2015): accessed July 10, 2018, https://warwick.ac.uk/fac/soc/economics/staff/dsgroi/impact/hp_briefing.pdf.

35.   Matt Smith, "How to be Happy (According to the World's Happiest Man)," *Esquire*, January 1, 2018, accessed July 10, 2018, https://www.esquire.com/uk/life/fitness-wellbeing/news/a4915/matthieu-ricard-what-ive-learned.

36.   Francesca Gino, "Are You Too Stressed to Be Productive? Or Not Stressed Enough?," *Harvard Business Review*, April 16, 2016, accessed July 10, 2018, https://hbr.org/2016/04/are-you-too-stressed-to-be-productive-or-not-stressed-enough.

Week Twenty-Two: Health and Productivity

37.   American Sleep Association, "Sleep and Sleep Disorder Statistics," accessed June 25, 2018, https://www.sleepassociation.org/about-sleep/sleep-statistics.

38.   D.S. Black, "Mindfulness Meditation and Improvement in Sleep Quality and Daytime Impairment Among Older Adults with Sleep Disturbances: A Randomized Clinical Trial," *JAMA Internal Medicine* 175, no. 4 (April 2015): 494–501, accessed June 25, 2018, https://doi.org/10.1001/jamainternmed.2014.8081.

39.   Carly M. Goldstein et al., "Current Perspectives on the Use of Meditation to Reduce Blood Pressure," *International Journal of Hypertension* (March 2012): accessed on April 5, 2018, http://dx.doi.org/10.1155/2012/578397.

40.   E.S. Epel et al., "Meditation and Vacation Effects Have an Impact on Disease-Associated Molecular Phenotypes," *Translational Psychiatry* 6 (August 2016): e880, accessed on June 25, 2018, https://doi.org/10.1038/tp.2016.164.

41.   Fadel Zeidan et al. "Mindfulness-Meditation-Based Pain Relief Is Not Mediated by Endogenous Opioids," *Journal of Neuroscience* 36, no. 11 (March 2016): 3391-3397, accessed April 5, 2018, https://doi.org/10.1523/JNEUROSCI.4328-15.2016.

Week Twenty-Seven: Gratitude

42.   Sara B. Algoe, Shelly L. Gable, and Natalya C. Maisel, "It's the little things: Everyday Gratitude as a Booster Shot for Romantic Relationships," *Personal Relationships* 17 (2010): 217–233, accessed August

9, 2018, https://greatergood.berkeley.edu/images/application_uploads/Algoe-GratitudeAndRomance.pdf.

43. Alex M. Wood et al., "Gratitude Influences Sleep through the Mechanism of Pre-Sleep Cognitions," *Journal of Psychosomatic Research* 66, no. 1 (January 2009): 43–48, accessed August 9, 2018, https://doi.org/10.1016/j.jpsychores.2008.09.002.

44. P.L. Hill, M. Allemand, and B.W. Roberts, "Examining the Pathways Between Gratitude and Self-Rated Physical Health across Adulthood," *Personality and Individual Differences* 54, no.1 (January 2013): 92-96, accessed August 9, 2018, https://dx.doi.org/10.1016%2Fj.paid.2012.08.011.

Week Twenty-Eight: Practicing Non-Judgment

45. Eckhart Tolle, *A New Earth* (New York: Plume, 2005), 61.

Week Thirty-Four: Mindfulness and Emotional Intelligence

46. Nicola S. Schutte and John M. Malouff, "Emotional intelligence Mediates the Relationship Between Mindfulness and Subjective Well-Being," *Personality and Individual Differences* 50, No. 7 (May 2011): 1116-1119, accessed June 21, 2018, https://doi.org/10.1016/j.paid.2011.01.037.

Week Thirty-Five: Meditation and Sleep

47. National Sleep Foundation, "2005 Sleep in America Poll," accessed June 25, 2018, https://sleepfoundation.org/sites/default/files/2005_summary_of_findings.pdf.

48. Black, "Sleep Quality," 494-501.

Week Thirty-Eight: Mindfulness Mediation and Creativity

49. Viviana Capurso, Franco Fabbro, and Cristiano Crescentini, "Mindful Creativity: The Influence of Mindfulness Meditation on Creative Thinking," *Frontiers in Psychology* 4 (2013): 1020, accessed on April 5, 2018, https://dx.doi.org/10.3389%2Ffpsyg.2013.01020.

50. Hugh Delahanty, "Does Meditation Boost Creativity?," *Mindful*, June 19, 2017, accessed April 5, 2018, https://www.mindful.org/does-meditation-boost-creativity.

Week Forty-Three: Awakening and Seeing
51. Hafiz, "We Might Have to Medicate You," *The Gift*, trans. Daniel Ladinsky (New York: Penguin Putnam, 1999), 217.
52. Walter Isaacson, *Steve Jobs* (New York: Simon and Shuster, 2011), 49.

Week Forty-Four: Chanting
53. B.G. Kalyani, G. Venkatasubramania, and R. Arasappa, "Neurohemodynamic Correlates of 'OM' Chanting: A Pilot Functional Magnetic Resonance Imaging Study," *International Journal of Yoga* 4, no. 1 (Jan 2011): 3-6, accessed May 24, 2018, https://doi.org/10.4103/0973-6131.78171.
54. Swami Jnaneshvara Bharati, "Maranatha: A Christian Meditation Mantra," accessed August 9, 2018, http://www.swamij.com/maranatha. htm.
55. Aryeh Kaplan, *Jewish Meditation* (New York: Schocken Books, 1985), 57.

Valentine's Day: Why Metta *Meditation Is So Good For You*
56. Cendra A. Hutcherson, Emma M. Seppala, and James J. Gross, "Loving-Kindness Meditation Increases Social Connectedness," *Emotion* 8, No. 5 (October 2008): 720-724, accessed June 25, 2018, https://doi.org/10.1037/a0013237.
57. Goleman, *Altered Traits*, 112.

Summer: Mindfulness Outdoors
58. A well-written summary of research can be found in this *Business Insider* article by Lauren F. Friedman and Kevin Loria, "11 Scientific Reasons You Should Be Spending More Time Outside," *Business Insider*, April 22, 2016, accessed June 29, 2018, https://www.businessinsider.com/scientific-benefits-of-nature-outdoors-2016-4.

Thanksgiving: Gratitude
59. For more information on these findings, see: Harvard Medical School, "In Praise of Gratitude," Harvard Health Publishing, November 2011, accessed January 30, 2018, https://www.health.harvard.edu/newsletter_article/in-praise-of-gratitude.

Appendix A; How to Create a Calm Room

60.   Jonathon S. Kaplan, "Plants Make You Feel Better," *Psychology Today*, March 11, 2009, accessed July 2, 2018, https://www.psychologytoday. com/us/blog/urban-mindfulness/200903/plants-make-you-feel-better.

ABOUT THE AUTHOR

Edie has a BA in Foreign Service and International Relations from Penn State University and an MA and PhD in Sociology from the University of Virginia. She has been a coach and consultant for Rewire since 2015, helping people and organizations find sustainable solutions for life and workplace success. She has taught yoga for over ten years, was named one of Baltimore's best yoga teachers in *Baltimore* Magazine, and is a co-founder of Off the Grid Yoga & Camping Retreats. She is the author of *Mussar Yoga*, a book connecting yoga and mindfulness with a traditional system of self-improvement. Edie diligently seeks a quieted mind through her daily practice of mindfulness meditation..

PHOTO CREDITS

Cover: Photo by Chris Barbalis on Unsplash
Page 15: Photo by David Zawila on Unsplash.
Page 17: Photo by Frank McKenna on Unsplash.
Page 19: Photo by Jeremy Bishop on Unsplash.
Page 21: Photo by Yoann Boyer on Unsplash.
Page 23: Photo by Le Minh Phuong on Unsplash.
Page 25: Photo by Ben White on Unsplash.
Page 29: Photo by Elijah M. Henderson on Unsplash.
Page 33: Photo by Jenn Evelyn Ann on Unsplash.
Page 35: Photo by Sanwal Deen on Unsplash.
Page 37: Photo by 童 彤 (@Liz99) on Unsplash.
Page 39: Photo by Matthew Henry on Unsplash.
Page 41: Photo by Isabell Winter on Unsplash.
Page 43: Photo by Andrew Seaman on Unsplash.
Page 45: Photo by Steven Spassov on Unsplash.
Page 47: Photo by Evan Kirby on Unsplash.
Page 51: Photo by Aaron Burden on Unsplash.
Page 55: Photo by Quino Al on Unsplash.
Page 57: Photo by Rawpixel on Unsplash.
Page 59: Photo by Rawpixel on Unsplash.
Page 61: Photo by Jony Ariadi on Unsplash.
Page 63: Photo by Kevin Ku on Unsplash.
Page 65: Photo by Benjamin Child on Unsplash.
Page 67: Photo by Adi Goldstein on Unsplash.
Page 69: Photo by Mikito Tateisi on Unsplash.
Page 73: Photo by Zac Durant on Unsplash.
Page 75: Photo by Nathan Dumlao on Unsplash.
Page 77: Photo by Bewakoof.com Official on Unsplash.
Page 79: Photo by Kitty Kouwenhoven.
Page 81: Photo by Sebastian Leon Prado on Unsplash.
Page 83: Photo by Simon Rae on Unsplash.
Page 85: Photo by Grant Ritchie on Unsplash.
Page 89: Photo by Rhema Kallian on Unsplash.

Page 91: Photo by Steven Houston on Unsplash.

Page 93: Photo by Rawpixel on Unsplash.

Page 95: Photo by Kelly Sikkema on Unsplash.

Page 97: Photo by Ruben Bagues on Unsplash.

Page 99: Photo by Lucy Chian on Unsplash.

Page 103: Photo by Jean Wimmerlin on Unsplash.

Page 107: Photo by Milos Prelevic on Unsplash.

Page 115: Photo by Mahir Uysal on Unsplash.

Page 119: Photo by Heather Zabriskie on Unsplash.

Page 121: Photo by Joshua Rawson Harris on Unsplash.

Page 123: Photo by Milada Vigerova on Unsplash.

Page 125: Photo by Anika Huizinga on Unsplash.

Page 129: Photo by Jerry Kiesewetter on Unsplash.

Page 131: Photo by Mark Tegethoff on Unsplash.

Page 133: Photo by Erik Witsoe on Unsplash.

Page 135: Photo by Kimson Doan on Unsplash.

Page 137: Photo by Stephanie McCabe on Unsplash.

Page 139: Photo by Tarik Haiga on Unsplash.

Page 141: Photo by Nils Stahl on Unsplash.

Page 143: Photo by Monika Grabkowska on Unsplash.

Page 145: Photo by Denys Nevozhai on Unsplash.

Page 154: Photo by Kitty Kouwenhoven.

Page 167: Photo by Kitty Kouwenhoven.

Made in the USA
San Bernardino, CA
15 October 2018